A Timeless Journey

a glimpse of possibilities

Karen Rhodes and
Marcelle Rhodes–Webster

Outskirts Press, Inc.
Denver, Colorado

Photography by Karen Rhodes and A. Marcelle Webster

Outskirts Press, Inc.
http://www.outskirtspress.com

ISBN: 978-1-4327-1648-6

Outskirts Press and the "OP" logo are trademarks belonging to Outskirts Press, Inc.

PRINTED IN THE UNITED STATES OF AMERICA

A Special Thank You

To all our family members; our many friends; our vast acquaintances, who have contributed to our journey of life, learning, and love on this plane – and the next.

Visit the Rhodes sisters at
www.RhodesJourney.com

Colorful Nightmare

by E.T. Webster

"Where I can hear angels calling out for help and intelligence causes insanity, leaving bliss far behind. I'm speaking of a place where dreamers want to be until they get there. It's like being in a drunken stooper and wishing nothing more than to be sober – and vise versa. Not realizing it doesn't matter the state of your physical mind, for the madness runs deeper than any chemical can reach. Not alcohol or ecstasy, not nicotine or ether. Nothing. Enough. Time to wake from this colorful nightmare. But alas – you realize you've been awake all along."

Table of Contents

Introduction

Truer words were never spoken than these – "the spirit is willing, but the flesh is weak."

My sister and I are sitting here on my redwood deck, located on the back of my old white farmhouse, watching my seven beautiful kittens frolic out on my twenty acres of wooded land. Life seems pretty good when we're alone and undisturbed.

We are writing and we feel good. All the excuses, all the guilt – seeps right out of us.

We make excuses everyday for not writing. We have to realize this is first in our lives. Maybe it is just an obsession. We hope not. We hope it is real – very real. But in either case, it doesn't really matter. If we finish this work we can go on with our lives and enjoy the large and small pleasures of this life.

So, everyone, find what you need to accomplish in this life – what you were sent here to do – finish it and move on. Otherwise, you will never feel complete. You will never enjoy life to the fullest until you have mastered your life's calling.

Our calling is this book.

We are haunted by feelings of need to start and finish a book – this book. We need to see if there is a chance that some people might open their minds and hearts to different ideas and thoughts, to question what was instilled in them during childhood, adolescents, adulthood, and to not accept what is supposedly true. Our desire is for you to open your minds to a very much larger picture, seeing with your hearts instead of your logic. Do not take everything we say as fact, but as a door to unleashing your own inner awareness, stirring up a cloud of dust in our minds and settling down to the task at hand. As the saying goes, "some things are true whether you believe them or not."

Where is this world going? Will it finally fall off its' axis from the weight of hatred and ignorance – drifting off eternally into space? Or, will it spring anew with love and patience.

The leaves are falling now. A gentle warm breeze is blowing them off the trees this lovely balmy autumn afternoon. The leaves are brown and dry. They seem useless. But they will, again, replenish the ground.

What comes again after winter springs life

anew. We, too, can become what we were sent here to do.

All it takes is a questioning of your belief system. Where did your belief system originate? Why do you incorporate certain guidelines into your life? Do you feel them to be authentic and undistorted? Why or why not?

Everyday mundane life is very arduous on a person, even if life here is satisfying. We all slip in and out of the spiritual world; however, it is more convenient to remain in our human existence where we can control most of our destiny. But alas, we miss out. We miss out on happiness. Our true contentment can only come from our spiritual dimension.

My sister and I are not writers, but we have a need to share our thoughts. Our spirits are just s–l–o–w–l–y prodding us along. Please, bear with us.

If you never question, how can you expect answers?

If you accept all answers, you never question.

What is a journey? Is it the time spent, aging, maturing, challenges met along the way?

No.

It is a series of moments. Most importantly, it is the moments you are not prepared for, and your reaction to them – both good and bad – the bigger the better. The more unexpected and unprepared moments, and how you deal with them, is how you truly define both yourself and your journey.

That's life. A journey. A series of moments.

The most defining and the most unexpected moments are, also, the most memorable moments. They are the reasons for living life. We experience love; loneliness; excitement; grief; hope; despair; moments of strength; moments of fear; experience of a new love; loss; birth; death – but what about the time in between? Is it to simply exist as a mundane passing of time?

We don't think so. Nor, is it a time to reflect on past moments, or to plan for the future ones.

Why?

The answer is because neither exists.

What does?

The answer is the now, the present.

Live by the adage, "seize the day", or you are not living at all. Better yet, "seize the moment". Live not in the past, nor plan for the future. In doing so, you can take away from the unanticipated that has not yet come to pass.

So, do what in between?

Make moments happen. Because, one day your time will come to pass, and it will enter unto someone else's series of moments.

Make it a memorable journey, and then it will all be worth it – including the unexpected.

Now, ask yourself, "Do I own this moment?" If the answer is no – *why not?*

We want to take you on a journey. A spiritual journey. You can decide if it's truth or fantasy. It really doesn't matter. But, it *will* give your spirit a lift. If at any point you recognize anything that pertains to you – stop – close your eyes and dwell on that thought for a few moments. You should receive some spiritual pleasure or satisfaction in the process.

Just remember this is only a test of your imagination, inner feelings and strength. Dare to think and create. Stagnation of the mind leads to disease and death. Let's not go there.

As you read this book, keep in mind that "time" – as we know it – is a creation of human man. Time cannot be measured. Time is infinite. The sequence of "time" has no beginning and it has no end.

Also keep in mind, this book is fiction – purely fiction – dreamt up by two attractive, vivacious, mature women. (Okay, writer's embellishment.) This is simply a roller coaster ride of emotions. So, buckle your seat belt. Or better yet, take off your complacent seat belt and enjoy the ride!

~ *What if?* ~

What if we came from a world that was so advanced and unrelated to this one? What if we came from a place where there is no sickness, fear or hate? What if we conducted experimental tests on different planets – planets that were created just for this purpose? Imagine these experiments being not your typical experiments with laboratory coats, rats and chemicals – but experiments of the heart.

What if we came from a world where we are testing our way from the inside out? Imagine taking an empty shell – a specimen – then transporting us one by one into these bodies or pods, leaving behind everything we hold dear. Imagine leaving behind our existence as we know it, hence, becoming a guide in this new vehicle so that we may live a lifetime here.

What if we were only limited to the ordination of ones' flesh?

Chapter 1

Beginnings

As I get up to walk towards the compound, I can feel the warmth of my mother's love. I stop, close my eyes, and bathe in the moment. Feeling refueled, I continue on my way.

Catching sight of the compound, it never ceases to amaze me of the majesty of the structure itself. The three gold spun peaks that are hand laced in silver seem to be floating in the clouds that lie above it. Gold beams shoot from every angle of the being, bringing out the rainbow of colors that lay in each and every brick, which every single brick is placed one by one and infused with life and love.

I come to rest at the foot of this enormous life force, rest my hand on the crimson brick and share a moment with this friend. Upon

1

entering, I remember knowing a small part in the excavating of the building and I feel those parts deep down inside me, as if I hold inside me a marble of light.

As I move down the corridor to the entrance, I feel the warmth of my being coming forth and encompassing the inhabitants, then receiving their warmth in return. I love coming to this place. The vibrations of the wheels turn within everyone, where you can make anything happen just by being.

Everyone looks extraordinary!

Working with such great intensity always makes me smile. I can feel something wonderful on the horizon and I want to know and experience more.

Michah, who is busy with detailing ongoing experiments, turns to welcome my curiosity. We hold hands and greet one another. I feel he wants to show me something so unlike anything we have ever done before. The stirring inside of me causes me to emanate joy. How exciting for everyone!

He takes me to a visual.

When our beings connect, he begins to show me what is in store – something I already know deep down inside. We blend our hearts and share a vision of what is to become. With all our god-force aglow we are as one. All hearts are one.

Our journey of love's experiments is to begin. We are about to stretch our love to all new heights, farther than we can ever imagine, seeing where and how it will come together and sending it out far beyond our universe to find out whether we can find our way home. Home. Home where our hearts will be – when it is time to return.

Our first mission is to assemble a planet that will adequately suit our plan, which will accommodate human pods without a soul entity. We will do a rough draft, carefully placing life forms in unpredictable elements. First and foremost we will call on all of our forces, focusing on every ounce of power we hold inside of us, producing love that we can project into lives unknown. Is love everything? Can we put it out there in small substances? Will it grow, or will it become stagnant – quietly slipping away?

We have our energy flowing, feeling every ounce of our god-force. We can never attempt anything like this without our force. We thank them for this opportunity of sharing – always sharing – feeling very blessed and peaceful.

Our work is being laid out. Most certainly we

will all help, small or large, it is all-equal. With every being of our god-lines, we spin balls of gases and solids until consolidated, creating seas and fossil-like life forms. Mastering our energy uniformly, we focus on this new plane we name "creation".

Next, the major continents form and begin to drift. We take much care and test several ice ages. Everyone has a hand in some life forms, which we name ourselves.

The scorpions are perhaps one of our first land animals. We all watch with such fervor as he crawls over the soft sand of what we call the "creation". The seas are developing organisms such as reef-building corals; nautiloids; amonoids; sharks. Moss animals appear, as do the vertebrates. Everything is changing and evolving into this new land. The mountain chains begin to become apparent. They rise further and further, upwards and outwards. A series of glaciating take place and vast swamps lead to the formation of coal beds. Then the first reptiles, whose embryos we develop, creep upon the dry land.

The "creation" becomes alive!

We feel as if it is transpiring right within the palms of our hands – evolving ever so rapidly.

Landforms continue to diversify, especially

insects and reptiles. Early mammal-like reptiles appear that will give rise to mammals. However, some life forms do not make it through the evolution. Perhaps, because we do not predict how high the seas will rise, nor how low the tides are to become. Some adventures we do not count on, therefore, I am sorry for the creatures or inhabitants that may suffer. Even a soulless vessel has a purpose and a reason.

From the reptiles, dinosaurs begin to form, as do, flying reptiles and fish-like reptiles. As this period ends, the first egg laying mammals arise, which are more indigenous to us.

Our imaginations are soaring!

The land begins to break away and islands are forming. My heart seems to be sailing. It is as if I am watching a small child grow and develop. Thus begins the ocean ways with a copious of islands and oceanic crystal plates. So many things are beginning and concluding.

Our plane is coming together magnificently!

Oh, the land creatures! We create some of the most extraordinary animals we can possibly dream of. We love these horrific creatures! They are larger than life itself. We exhaust all we have into them, the lizards, the birds, each evolving from the beginning.

Shallow seas expand from themselves and growing mountain chains begin to appear.

As the last of the dinosaurs come forth, we feel we are out of control. *We feel as if we have misstep.*

Boundaries are beginning that we do not expect. The human forms that are evolving are not as we anticipated. It is kill or be killed – total chaos. Even without souls, we calculate in some form of love, some commiseration. What has gone awry? We pour everything we have into this project. Maybe it is not enough.

We will have to abandon ship!

Nonetheless, if we do abandon ship we will most definitely try again. We cannot allow this massive and glorious body of land and sea to be in vain. But if we do try again, we can never do it in the same manner.

Upon ending this existence, we will need to recycle and replenish the plane again.

Resulting from the consultation of counsel, we are sending a massive asteroid to collide with creation, allowing it to open up and swallow its inhabitants. We will now have to start from the beginning, the *very* beginning.

Again, darkness inhabits the plane. It is without configuration or light. We must bring forth light, light from love and expressions from our beings. Our god-force must be laced in every form of breath, light and love. It must be a total connection from the largest of creatures to the smallest of creatures, from the mountains to the seas. Every form of life must be connected – all one.

Our vessels on this next journey have to be impeccable. They cannot derive from the land. There will be no evolution this time. We will each take a piece of ourselves, our most treasured attributes that are given from on high, which have the most lasting impressions. We have no idea how long this adventure will last, or where it will take us. We have tried similar projects in various universes, but not like this one. There is an oddly familiar feeling to this plane, very much like our own world. And this time we will see it through – no stopping – even if we encounter setbacks. We will work through the unexpected.

There is no turning back now. We can feel the vibrations from within us all. Connecting, transpiring, breaking free.

Freewill, what will we do with it? We know it; we feel it, but to truly let it go, to let it fly – sensational!

Our vessels will need to be self-proficient. If a bacterium enters in, the heart will send a message to the brain that will cause the temperature to rise and flame out the "intruder". If the outer layer of epidermis is punctured or split, all the cells will be working together to repair the damage. Every cell and every organ will be willing to grow anew, just by a thought process – through the heart – onto the brain – then to the problem.

Each vessel will be equipped with a protective light encircling the body that will not allow intrusive entrance, unless invited. The brain will work in connection to the heart. It will house our temperaments, our feelings and our thoughts – transpiring, holding and projecting them, but exclusively connected through the heart where the blood and life flows.

The heart can send thoughts through the brain that can change the whole molecular structure of our being for healing, for stimulation, or for advancement.

The healing powers are very important. If the vessels are taken care of properly by feeding the heart and mind, they will be indestructible. No outside power can tamper them.

You will find food and nourishment all around you. The healing will come from inside of you, and from the earth and air. The roots and leaves of the dandelion will remedy a multitude of needs. The more you cultivate this plane, the more you will receive. Also, look to the golden seal, echinacea and ephedra, the wind will be your guide. Go to the earth to feed the hungry and maintain the wholeness of your spirit. What may seem to be insignificant could be your food for the day.

The energy that we are accustomed to in our homeland will not be seen by the bare eye. The rainbow in the atmosphere will remind us of all the diverse colors of strength that flows through our bodies. Tones from the frequency of the hues will connect every living being, and every object that has been touched by a being, including thoughts. Parts of our energy will remain here long after we have departed this foreign homestead. Even though only some will know and be able to recognize these pieces, we are still all connected in this life. We may meet a "stranger" and have a strong connection, not knowing exactly why. It is that the same timbre flows through us, a connection we both shared at home.

In addition, we must create an existence of negativity since we are to be in a natural state. This state of mind will have to swing in every aspect of consciousness, thus making its' own evolving trip. However, this entity of negativity can only invade our awareness by permission from above, giving it very little power (but still being an obstacle to contend with), which prompts me to wonder how it will grow in time.

For mating or for reproduction we will have to furnish organs that are similar to the animal world, yet, much more complex. This is very technical, since we – the sculptors – have both male and female qualities.

We will have to split these qualities in half in order to procreate in a natural environment, while at the same time, wondering if the split will send one or the other looking for their lost attributes. The body's stress supply will be held in the sexual organs and then released at the time of impulse.

The entire mating ritual will be filled with pleasures abound. Every couple who indulges in their pleasures will exchange a small piece of one another souls and incorporate it into their own personality, be it a negative or positive energy, to hold with them for this life's journey. Furthermore, pieces of one another souls will grow in our own offspring for generations to come.

We are anxiously curious as to the outcome of the male/female separation of qualities. How will the two react to their own unique makeup?

Will there be resentment – attraction – acceptance? We will have to wait and see.

Albeit, we are slightly concerned with the male species having physically strong attributes (not necessarily stronger than his counter part). Will the species be more closely related to the animal world? Which way will he lean towards, the human existence or the animal existence? Without his mothering counterpart to guide him, will he venture towards being like his evolutionary brother? We know it is a possibility. Only time will tell. Maybe he will find his mother ship amidst the darkness and find his way home again. And too, he will still have his female alter ego with him that holds all his inward strengths and qualities. He can always depend on that to fulfill all his needs. That just might be the energy needed.

The female extraction will hold all the mothering skills of a great wild animal. She will be the force that keeps the world together. Her strength will be found in the eyes of her offspring. She will carry her young in the belly of her womb, bringing forth child with pain and joy, caring for them greatly in their young years, and then sending them out into the world as do the animals, sending them on their way to make their own life on this plane.

By coming forth to procreate, the female and male entities should be very wary of filling their offspring with their own individual ideologies and fears of this existence, because every being's path will be different.

Paths may cross, but paths seldom run in the same direction.

We must put love first. Only when we put love first, will everyone and everything fall into its' orderly place. Offspring are just borrowed beings who should be taken care of in no certain manner. They should be held lovingly, but not too closely, so they may ride out their own lives on this plane.

We must forgive each and every step of the way, letting go of unresolved differences. Also, we should not hang on to any human bondage that could anchor onto our souls.

Will we lean toward our human identities that can weigh us down and drag us back to this new plane? Or, will we soar like the birds above our heads, letting our spirit guide and nurture this vessel of bondage, breaking free at the end of our journey knowing what we have achieved and knowing what we can learn from this existence we will call home for ages to come?

Our goal is to view and understand the ability to have our existence become a reality on the new plane. Will love take the tiniest of vessel and blend them together with every inhabitant? Or, will survival prevail and our mission be fruitless? Or yet, will a new view submerge and grow to become a reality, a brand new part of oneself?

The thought itself astounds my being! Growing – hopefully, continuously growing with connected viability.

We make every effort to achieve this fulfillment with the ability to return on several journeys to this plane. Whether the number of trips is one, fifty-one or a hundred and one, the pilots will always choose them and their ability to accept renewal, letting the force of our godliness be our commander.

We number the days of this existence to avoid getting caught up in this experience of life, and fail to return home – which is always a possibility. On this new plane our memory banks will be null and void of any recollection of what we are or of what we are to become – which can prove to be highly complicated. Of course, we will never be alone. Still, we may choose to be alone if the experience calls for it to be so.

We may choose to be who and what we are to become, such as, body types; personality; origin. More significantly, we may choose the obstacles that we encounter, where the life's lessons will be found.

We set up a system of affinity with our universe and with the new plane. A system where our energy of godliness lives in an analogy based world just parallel to the new plane. We will be able to touch and call upon our spiritual guides for help and well being, even though, we won't always be able to see them with the human eye. We can talk to them with our hearts and listen with our inner ear, crossing over with a breath, but not knowing where we have been.

Refueling and working out details will come in the unconsciousness. When the plane is dark and the "creation" is sleeping, then will we return to our dimension to survey our intentions and purpose, reaching out for help with connected recognition that is just a touch away.

The freedom of the vessel will take on journeys of its' own, not knowing where one is going or where one will end up. The stories that we share when we return will always be remembered and will always burn true in our beings.

As we are making our final preparations for this grand voyage, our higher counsel gathers us together for some final words of wisdom and encouragement.

"Everything you need to know to survive this existence is contained in your spirit, from the god specter to the smallest of insect – the knowledge is contained in these. Nonetheless, it must be sought after and longed for. So, you must look into yourselves and discover the reasoning for your travels. You will have it with you from the moment you squeeze from your mother's womb, and you will return with your insight when you make your voyage home again.

Each vessel will contain your own set of similarities, such as, personalities; likes and dislikes; compatibility ratio. As a result, you will have human obstacles to conquer with spirit fulfillment. Some may decide later to re-enter a vessel, to re-enact a life that didn't turn out to be satisfactory, in order that you may absorb the experience completely. When you find the path that fulfills your journey – peace, joy and wisdom shall follow you the rest or your days – which are timeless.

From the trees, to the soil, to the larvae that crawls beneath the soil, to the human that walks upon the soil – all is connected. One cannot survive without the other. From the air we all breathe to the godliness we all share, from the largest to the smallest – all must be respected, as in our homeland.

Find pride and acceptance as you watch the small lizard sun himself and raise his tiny arm to rest it on his back. There you will find the most pleasures of the day. Not knowing of the lizard before this day, but knowing you are connected. Respect for your "creation" will bring forth fruit and abundance.

All creatures large and small contain water. Water is your life force here on this plane. Treat this with the utmost care, as you will do with the air and the land. All is as one. One without the other will not suffice. The responsibility of this plane is in the hands of the human – all human – all one. Take care of each other and all inhabitants, for you may find yourself in the eyes of anyone of them someday.

The body will be equipped with everything it will need for this journey. If you can think it, it will be done. However, be ever so careful of what you may wish for, for in time it will be yours.

Moreover, what comes from your mouths

should be pure, for once you say it, it will become yours. The power is within oneself. You carry it with you always. What you give to others you will receive in return, good or bad. Likewise, be careful that the unsteadiness of this life does not turn into fear. For what is fear? Fear of whom or what? Fear of losing this body? Fear of this existence? Don't walk in fear, nor run from it. Your protection is always there. You are never alone.

Energy flows through all that has life. Energy is not visible to the naked eye, just as this new sphere of existence is being cared for by beings not visible to the naked eye yet; they are there nonetheless. Nature's children from above will come forth in many forms, seen and not seen, taking pride in working and protecting the natural wonders of the new plane.

Enjoy each of these journeys. Do not suffer long, for in the deliverance of pain you will find happiness and strength. Study from all the masters that will be before you and after you. Do not allow a fellow being profess to you what your mission is to be on this new plane. You may be advised, but only you and your forces must find your path to follow.

May your journeys begin and end with love,

first and foremost. Remember love prevails when everything else fails. Love is what you know when you first enter this "creation" and it is what you will know when you step from this plane to your home. What you fill it up with will be up to your purpose and your needs. Finding your way back home may not be as easy as you think, but if you can bring about the love that we share here and manifest it on this plane, your trips shall not be in vain."

I can feel the dissention of my siblings to this plane. A small piece of me is aching, but the greatest part of me is abounding with joy. I wish you all a soul so full of joy that life's weathering storms can not destroy it.

Chapter 2

Dusk of New Beginnings

I stand here ready to view the lives from which I can choose. There is torment, love and justice hidden in each of them. I will sit with my guide and we can discuss my choice.

It is difficult to leave home.

I know I will still have my attachment here, but will I be aware of it? Will I remember, or will I drift aimlessly? Or sadly enough – will I cling to the world in which I am alien?

I can choose my fate, rest assured of bringing back much knowledge and tales of inspiration, which every level of godliness will know and incorporate.

My guide approaches. I see the light radiating from his being – and from mine. I see the love and the connection between this life and the next life. I see my quest I have chosen. I sit and play it through as it encircles my being, preparing to coalesce.

My guide waits in front of me. Each and every one of my family members has chosen words to help me pass, but beneath the surface I feel the pulling of our hearts, for our hearts are all tied together. They share with me these thoughts:

"You will see our presence in every walk of life. What we once shared will become apparent in every nation. The tales of ancestry will be very similar and the endings will all hold the same truths. So, don't hold too tight to the story, for the tale is only your guide. Grab hold of the unknown, for this is your way back home. Look hard and true to find the clues – the clues that are buried inside of you, inside of us. We are all one. Your strengths will come from within. All wisdom will come from where we hide deep inside of you. We lie ready to be awakened, ready to draw anew. Don't ever feel small or inferior, because the fire in you is greater than what you see or feel. Remember, when your soul leaves to return back home, it shall remain the same — whole and untouched by this life's aggressions. Hold on to that, and that alone. When the key fits it will fit exact and true. Go with all your journeys into the unknown. Dark is your light; night is your day. Slip through and awaken on a new plane."

The Journey...

I'm just beginning on this new plane. It is my first voyage. Fear is not a factor. I am able to see with my eyes and my original celestial sphere.

My nurturers I left behind are diligently watching me from the clouds. At first, I believe all the populace that is here with me, sees their existence correlating with their true home. Yet, the longer I am here I realize not all the inhabitants can travel to and fro. So, I have come to believe that they must have wanted it that way. As for this moment, I appreciate having the ability to call upon my kinsman whenever needed. As a being walks up and down stairs, we are able to go back and forth from this plane to our original homeland, albeit, *only* in spirit.

I'm not sure how many of us have the capability to do this, but I can find out when our forefathers and mothers return for guidance, even when it is not solely for my own purpose. We fanatically secure our presence in this region.

We are given a great society of overseers that live in a realm of their own. We visualize their society and learn lessons, as well as acquire knowledge from every source of their activities. They are a great society of gods and monarchy of which I have chosen to become entwined (in short intervals.)

Surely, the tales from these magnificent god-like creatures will be used for generations to come. They are great rulers of our sky, protectors of our plane, and they govern our seas. They bring us many gifts, music; poetry; spoken word. Different, nonetheless similar in nature, to what we shared in our true state. They are helping us to build monuments of force and energy with the aid of our siblings from back home. These monuments serve as a place of escape for us. It is a place where our spirits can be filled with the light of the heavens, which is our power source we left behind when we entered this atmosphere.

They are bringing to this land, materials from distant shores of our homeland. Care is being taken in precise measurements. All eyes cannot see these monuments of light. It is only for the ones that seek its' power. Their spirit will let them know where it is located, for they are hidden in the very remote parts of the desert land – where the sands turn as white as light.

The secrets will live only within us, never to be discussed openly. The secrets will remain in us for the duration of every journey on this plane.

It is very rewarding to be a help to both sides in preparing these towers of illumination. The requirements for this mysterious vessel have to be relevant to everything we shared before. The thirteen acres this vessel covers, comes from the number of planets we have inhabited – including this plane. The sides, roughly seven hundred and fifty-five feet long, is the number of star planets we abide in. On the outside, at the feet of the buildings, lies a great lion of crystal radiance. It resembles the power of our invisible protection that remains with us for eternity. We can see him with our spirits, but if we were to touch him, our hands would pass directly through him.

On the inside are long corridors made up of different shades of brilliance that pass through our bodies and are picked up by our souls, comparable to our birth experience on this venture.

The vessel opens up to a large chamber with a sepulcher. Whoever wishes, may place their mortal body in the sepulcher and be transported back to our authentic homeland.

This can only happen with the purest of beings. It is here that we can learn to live in both worlds with unlimited characteristics. We are taking great pride in cleansing and preparing these pods for travel. We are amongst a secret society that seems to be diminishing with each passing year.

At first, I believed us to be the only culture on this plane to have such a community. But now, I hear tales from afar and from our overseers. The tales are of different origins that have built similar vessels of light from on high. They, too, have come upon problems of greed and ignorance. Some have tried to die here and take with them their fortunes they have gained on this plane. Jewels and treasures. What purpose would they have in our homeland? I don't understand this want. Don't they remember where they came from? Don't they remember to where they are returning? Oh, the love that is lost here! We only rapture these bodies to test for imperfections. The ashes will be sprinkled out into the heavens and returned to this port. It is a travesty to believe they now wish to relocate their rubbish they have acquired here on this plane. Furthermore, when they reach home they will ultimately realize what nonsense it all was.

What has happened here deeply saddens me.

The morning of this day is the saddest day on this plane. I awoke early this morning not feeling my spiritual connections. I run outside to find there are no more overseers. The clouds have swallowed them up. My homeland is no longer visible to my eye. I run to the desert and to my great dismay, our monuments have been covered with water and mud. They are covered with a consistency that has turned them into rock – an impenetrable rock – that also covers our beast. Unrecognizable now, our lion is stripped of his pride.

I weep in this empty tomb. My tears bounce from the hard flooring.

No connections – just the small still voice of my spirit echoing deep within my being. The echo is fervently trying to connect into the wide black hole of my soul.

My memory is fleeting. Will I be able to remember the world I left behind, the world in which one foot still remains? I can only remember it through my heart, not through my memory or my eyes, but only through my heart.

I lift my hand and examine it closely. I can

see it slowly fading – slowly disappearing. Inside the core of my being, I am aware that I am not really here. Didn't we formulate this existence to be "mortal", to learn without a recollection of our genuine divine life? We sailed through this dream with minimal help and with our memory banks erased. Our spirit is contained in an organ that is disconnected of physical and spirit. Didn't we do this to see how strong we can be on our own, wanting to see if our spirits (our true beings) can conquer this physical state, tucking it neatly in a pouch to take it back home?

Yet, why would a world of perfect existence want to know a simpler state of mind? It has to connect in some way. I search my mind for the smallest remembrance.

It's disappearing.

My soul cries out a drop of knowing. Just as I am connected to the greenery that surrounds me, I am connected to you. You are in me and I am in you.

Nothing can change that, nothing here – nothing there. You can't change something that was always there and always will be. You can decide whether to tap into it or not, but what remains the same is always there. It is non-removed. No matter where we are, you will find us. We will find each other.

I stand up; realizing at this moment what brought about this fate. Again, delving into our immortality and not realizing our boundaries that we instilled together – greed and demise – aren't we foolish?

Suddenly I understand why my thoughts and anguish have brought me to this sepulcher these last few days. It was apparently for my journey home. My spirit ties are too strong to allow me to remain while I am still so attached.

I lie and wait for my removal from this plane.

⌘　　⌘　　⌘　　⌘

As I lie here awaiting my departure, I sense the coolness coming from the newly conformed rocks. An overwhelming feeling of iciness reminds me of the direction our new plane is taking. It is an unforeseen directive. We are slipping, making inevitable mistakes. I wonder how this will affect our next roles on this plane. Will our past indiscretions in this life change the outcome in our next adventure? And if so, how many generations will be inflicted by the blunders of the blind that led before them?

I cannot contemplate all the implications at this time. My thoughts are exhausting as I find myself swirling in memories – memories that are akin to a dancing white flame encircling my mind and body. Visions of living; visions of loving; visions of leaving. I will miss this home and I will be missed.

As my expedition leads me home, I have strong feelings of never leaving at all.

Was it a dream? A good dream, maybe. Part nightmare? Maybe. But at last, a still slumber of events that I had control over.

Or, in fact, no control over.

As I hang in the midst of this life and the

next, I feel an emptiness and confusion. I am not home and I am somnolent – hanging in the balance – weighing each moment with fervent intensity.

Chapter 3

Spiritual Void

Rapidly taking on another journey leaves me still confused and empty. My thoughts are vague and distorted. I am apprehensive, yet, tranquil.

I am erratically indifferent.

Despite not knowing the intent of my journey, I am overcome with a lethargic enfolding.

Where is this taking me? What is my purpose for being?

Am I alone?

The Journey...

Sometimes I just feel so stupid. Sometimes – most of the time – I hate myself, and everyone and everything. Being in trouble seems to be becoming my daily routine. I try, at times, to conform to the rules imposed on me by my parents and teachers, but then something goes off in my head and I do something so stupid.

It doesn't help being the youngest son, especially when my two older brothers never seem to do anything wrong. It's almost as if I subconsciously try to sabotage my "perfect" family lifestyle. I really don't believe I disrupt our lifestyle on purpose. I just have this uncontrollable force inside of me that takes over command of my actions.

There really is a part of me that wants to do the right thing. I truly always regret my bad choices, not only because I always get caught, but also because I sincerely want to be a good person.

It did help me feel a little bit better about myself when I was diagnosed with a reason for my behavior. Finally, for the first time in my life, I realize I am not crazy. The medication aids me in controlling my hyperactivity and impulsive behavior – when I choose to take the medication. However, most of the time I lie to my mother about taking my medication. I don't like how it alters my personality and my way of thinking. I can't explain it. I simply don't like the medication.

So, here I am. In trouble…again.

It looks like I am on the verge of getting kicked out of school for the third time. My dad, for all intended purposes, has washed his hands clean of me. My mother is becoming extremely frustrated. She is hanging on by a thread. Finding a school to send me to is becoming a problem. Their options are dwindling fast.

Even though I genuinely feel sorry for my mother, I delight in the power I seem to have lorded over my parents. They apparently have lost all control over me. On one hand, I enjoy my sense of freedom and my power of self-control. But strangely, on the other hand, I feel scared and insecure.

I am so lost and confused.

This was a big one this time. I got kicked out of school for smoking dope. Alcohol wasn't good enough. I needed something more powerful to tamper my brain. Drinking and getting high helps me feel more confident. I know that I appear to others as being tough, but if they could actually see inside of me, they would realize how scared and insecure I really am.

I can't allow anyone to know the truth, particularly myself. Therefore, it is a vicious cycle. The drinking and the drugs assists me in feeling secure – or numbs me to my feelings of insecurity – but then the physical harm of the drinking and the drugs scare me to death.

I am so terrified of dying.

I am seventeen years old now. I have completely dropped out of high school several months ago. I can't hold onto a job, partly because I have graduated on to more powerful drugs. My buddies and I seem to find it easier to steal things and pawn them for drug money, rather than hold on to a steady job.

I don't know what I'll do after my next birthday comes around. My parents say I have to leave the house if I don't have any direction in my life by the time I turn eighteen. They are worn down and they are tired of me overturning their lives. They are tired of their possessions turning up missing. They are tired of worrying what will become of me.

Being eighteen years old and out on my own is not what I expected it to be. I don't have a place to call home. Home is flopping down (all drugged up) on the sofa of anyone who will take me in for the night. My worldly possessions consist of a plastic garbage bag filled with a few items of clothing. The drugs control me – I no longer have control over myself. I telephone home every few days just to let my family know I am still alive. My buddies and I wake up in the middle of the afternoon to go pawn whatever we stole the night before; in order to buy tonight's drugs.

And so it goes.

Tonight's "job" is the tool shed in the backyard of an elderly couple. No problem, an easy prey.

Severing the lock off the door of the tool shed – there they are – the flaming blues lights. We try to run, but we are trapped by the fenced yard.

Being arrested and booked is not a new

experience for me. I was arrested once before on a minor charge and I was placed on probation, which makes this arrest much more frightening. I am still serving probation on the minor charge, so, I know I will not be able to bond out - not that my parents *would* bond me out a second time.

This small county jail is severely overcrowded. There are nine cellmates in this cell that is built for four people. Five guys are sleeping on the cold hard floor, of which I am one of them. The combination of stench between the nasty sweaty bodies and the cleaning chemicals is unbearable. The cell doors are open from 6:00 a.m. until 10:00 p.m., with little or no supervision. It is a powder keg of emotions exploding with the least hint of a spark. There is no outdoor activity here. Some guys have been here for a year or more, without seeing the light of day.

I try to keep to myself and mind my own business in here, but that is not always an easy thing to do, especially when you have vent up angry bullies just looking for an excuse to erupt on you.

Tonight was my night to get erupted on.

Brad, an incredibly major jackass, has had an unknown beef with me ever since I arrived in this sewer pit. He chose tonight, of all nights, to make good on his threats. Now tonight, the night before I go before the judge, I have this undeniable bulging black eye.

"How did you get that shiner?" the judge demands.

With my head bowed I murmur, "I hit the corner of the television in the sitting room."

"Speak up, and look at me when I'm talking to you," the judge bellows.

"I hit the corner of the television in the sitting room," I repeat.

"Yeah, right," he answers sarcastically. "That little lie just cost you your bond."

And with that he set my court date, almost two months from today.

The withdrawal from the drugs is beginning to take affect on me. Some days are better than others. Today is not so bad. What is bad is the monotony from one day to the next. The mindless conversations and the mindless television shows are about to drive me insane. This past month and twenty-two days has urged me to think about the path my life has taken. I don't want to be like these idiots in here. Now that I'm looking at my life with an unclouded view, my so-called friends are really beginning to sicken me. I can't stand to look at them any longer.

I just want out of this place!

I wish I could run as far away from this place as I can get, leaving behind everyone I know. How I would love to go to a brand new town where I know absolutely nobody and begin my life all over again.

But, it doesn't look like that is going to happen anytime soon.

Peering through the tiny window in the side door, I can see the courtroom is packed to capacity this morning. I keep trying to catch a glimpse of the crowd to see if my parents are out there. There are twelve of us "cellies" out here in the hallway, dressed in our orange jumpsuits and chains, waiting for our turn to go in before the judge. I hear the judge call my name. The jailer ushers me through the door, as I try and shuffle my way to the front of the courtroom. I spot my mother sitting in the third row. I muster up a reassuring glance to let her know everything will be all right.

After all the legal formalities are finished, the judge declares, "Eleven months and twenty-nine days." I turn to look at my mother and see that she is fighting back tears. I wish I could let her know that I am okay with the judge's decision. I really was expecting my sentence to be a whole lot worse.

I finally got my chance at the pay phone this evening. I just want my mother to know that I am fine. I also want to let her know that they will probably be shipping me out to a nearby state penitentiary to serve out my time. She really gets upset when she hears the news, but I assure her that it has got to be a lot better than being stuck in this county jail. At least I will have my own bed and I will be able to go outside to get some fresh air. Not only am I trying to reassure my mother, I am also trying to reassure myself.

I am scared to death.

I can handle this local county jail. Man, I know most of the guys in here. But prison – that is a whole different experience.

Getting settled in isn't as bad as I thought it would be. My "cellie" is a cool guy. He's an older man, married with two teenage girls. Also, he is a trustee. He has been teaching me the ropes; explaining all the procedures and letting me know which guys to stay clear of. It's almost reminiscent of high school. You have your variety of clicks here. There are the redneck skinheads, the blacks, the Mexicans, the gays, and the losers. If you just keep to yourself and stay away from the gangs, it really isn't all that bad.

I try to keep myself busy, so I don't have to think about things. I go to the workout room, I play basketball outdoors and I have even been reading a lot – something I have never done before. Also, they have me taking GED classes. They won't let you out of here unless you have a high school diploma. Still, it is difficult filling up your day. One day just seems to blend into the next day.

I look forward to visitation day. Mother visits me every Saturday and stays all day. We usually spend the day playing card games. Funny how all my so-called friends have seemed to have forgotten about me.

Seven months in this place and I am finally getting loose! I was told I probably wouldn't have to serve my entire time, and "they" were right. I feel as if I have a fresh lease on life – no drugs, no idiot friends, and a high school diploma to boot. I am ready to begin life all over again. My parents are even allowing me to come home, if I get a job and keep my nose clean.

If you think I have it made, well, you'd be wrong.

I did find a job and I did keep my nose clean – for about two weeks. But knowing I have money in my pocket only entices me to go buy a fix. I simply cannot handle this life. I'm scared, I'm angry, I'm confused, and I'm bored. *I hate life and I hate myself.*

⌘　　⌘　　⌘　　⌘

What did that all mean? Was it a dream? A good dream, maybe. Part nightmare? Maybe. A still slumber of events that I had control over. Or, in fact, no control over.

Where is my connection?

Where is my spirit?

Chapter 4

Staying Connected

The eradication of the beings from our former "creation" still has a fascinating effect on me. I am intrigued by the current make-up of the male species. How different is this species compared to the beings we first created?

Our soul, our lifeline, permeates our every connection. Knowing this, how will the most basic male species compare to our complete beings? Will he more closely resemble our first creations? Or, will he be more whole, more absolute, closely resembling our beings?

The blueprints are laid out, keeping in mind my fascination of our previous world.

I descend upon my journey into the questionable unknown, an experiment of trepidation. Yet, a journey agreed upon by all.

The Journey...

Twinkling "snow fairies" are dancing in my head. Am I in dreamland, or am I awake? I pull my pale blue blanket with the silk binding up under my chin. My eyelids begin to flutter. I try to pull them apart, but my eyelashes are glued shut with morning "sleep".

Daylight begins to stream through my eyes, as I force my eyelids open. I lie here in my little single wrought iron bed and look out the window across the room. "Jack Frost" has left icicles outside my window!

I shoot straight up in bed!

This is the big day!

I fly out of bed and run down the hallway, pulling up the droopy bottoms of my flannel pajamas. I burst into the bedroom of my two older sisters.

"Get up!" I scream. "Today's the day!"

I race like the wind back down the hallway, tripping over my small and clumsy feet. Debbie and Donna erupt with laughter.

"Wait, Danny," yells Donna. "Let's first wake up mom and dad."

We all three run to the other end of the house towards mom and dad's bedroom.

Before we reach their room, their bedroom door creeps open. Mom and dad groggily walk through the door, each tying the rope belts of their robes around their waists.

"Hey, what's going on?" bellows dad.

In unison we all three shout, "Today's the day!"

"It is?" laughs mom. "Well, what do you know?"

Mom heads to the kitchen to plug in the coffeepot. The three of us push and shove our way towards the overly decorated tree in the corner of the living room. Dad follows leisurely behind us and flops himself down on the sofa.

"Someone turn on the television," says dad boisterously. "I want to catch the news."

Donna immediately and obediently jumps over to the television set and turns it on.

Oblivious to the rest of our surroundings, Debbie and I plunge into the mound of colorful presents scattered beneath the tree.

I am so excited, I can barely breathe. Shredding the paper apart as fast as I can, I open my first present. *Building blocks!*

I hastily stumble over to the sofa. "Look, dad!" "Look what I got!"

"Yeah, go show your mom," he answers uninterestedly.

I cannot understand why dad is not as excited about today as I am. How can anyone not be so excited about the happiest day of the year? Maybe it is because parents don't get as many gifts as children do. Oh well, I can't think about that right now.

I run to the kitchen to show mom my building blocks.

"Well, how about that," mom smiles down at me very sweetly. "Aren't you a lucky little man, Danny?"

Mom follows me back out into the living room, carrying two cups of coffee. She hands dad one cup and sits down in her favorite chair.

Not a moment later has mom sat down, when dad screams at the top of his lungs.

Everyone jumps.

Mom leaps from her chair. "What?" "What is it?" she asks shakily.

"Ah, you're coffee is too hot. I just burnt my lip," barks dad.

Mom closes her eyes and lets out an audible sigh of relief, and sits back down in her chair.

Donna, Debbie and I have already forged on ahead into opening our presents. We were all quite used to being startled by dad's uncontrollable outbursts. Like mom, we were just relieved it was no more than a verbal outburst.

Mom went to her bedroom and came out with her box camera, and began taking pictures of us all. It is amazing how the photographs always capture the serenity of the "perfect average family". No one can ever see what lives beyond the mask of the lens – except those of us who live it.

Today turned out to be a very good day. My sisters and I received a lot of toys, and other swell presents. We played quietly most of the day, just basking in the joy and peacefulness that this day faithfully delivers every year.

Later on in the day, Grandma and Grandpa came over with more gifts. They then joined us for a scrumptious, and amazingly serene, dinner. Dad and Grandpa hardly even yelled. I think I only counted three arguments today.

I snuggle down in my little bed this evening and I pull my pale blue blanket with the silk binding up under my chin. Looking out my window across my bedroom, I can see the snow glitter under the moonlight.

Yes, this is one of my favorite days. I wish every day were like today!

It is late Saturday afternoon and dad is all

dressed up, standing behind the bar making some colorful drinks for mom and him. Mom is in her bedroom finishing getting ready for the evening. She told us earlier that she and dad were going to a cocktail party tonight and that Kathy will be babysitting for us. Kathy is the teenage girl who lives across the street.

A few minutes later mom comes out of the bedroom and joins dad at the bar. She looks so pretty in her frilly dress and sparkling jewelry. Mom begins to recite to us the familiar rules as she and dad both sip on their colorful drinks. Take a bath; put on your pajamas; mind the babysitter, etc.

We love it when Kathy is babysitting for us. We can all laugh and play as loud as we care to. We don't have to worry about saying the wrong thing and getting smacked in the face. We don't have to worry about getting told how stupid we are. We don't have to be careful about being too loud and upsetting dad. We don't have to worry about getting spanked with his big leather belt.

All we have to think about is having fun!

And have fun, we do! We play outside until the streetlights come on. Kathy even joins us in a couple of outdoor games.

I am so tired after I bathe and put on my

pajamas, that I don't even mind it when Kathy says it is bedtime.

Later this night, after I am fast asleep, I am awakening by angry voices coming from the living room. Familiar angry voices. Moderately loud – escalating louder.

I pull my pale blue blanket with the silk binding up over my head. *"Please, no - not again."*

I know my pleas are useless. I know it won't stop.

Dad's voice is getting louder. Mom's voice is getting softer, quietly begging him to calm down. But, as usual, it is as if she can't be heard.

"I hear you, mom."

Then, like clockwork, I hear the horrible name-calling. I hear the thunderous cracking of dad's blows.

I hear mom's cries and pleas growing louder.

"Please, Bill!" "Please, stop!" "The children!"

I wish I can help you, mom. Oh how I wish I can help you. But sadly, all I can do is lie here rigidly in my little bed and cry a silent tear for you, praying you will be okay.

After all the sounds are gone, I try to fall back to sleep. I keep wondering if Donna and

Debbie can hear what I hear so many nights while I lie here in my little bed. I want to ask them, but I am afraid to ask them.

As the years go by, the fights seem to have dwindled down. Perhaps they just got better at hiding them, the older we have become.

I am seventeen years old, now. The relationship between my dad and I has gotten even worse. Over the years I have grown to truly despise the man. I despise him to the point that I wish he were dead.

Not only have I grown to despise my dad, but I have also grown to despise my mom. I have no respect for a mother who would tolerate such abuse for so many years. How can I respect a mother who would not protect her own children? I used to think my mom really loved us.

But that's not love.

If she really loved us, she would have gathered us and sheltered us from our dad's violent physical and mental abuse, as well as herself. If she really loved us; she would not have cared about losing her home and her security in material possessions. To me, she is just as selfish as my dad is.

It is very difficult being a teenager. I find myself following the wrong crowd, getting into trouble at home, and even having minor scrapes with the law.

I drink too much, like my dad.

I never wanted to be like my dad, but I find myself being more and more like him everyday. I have so much anger pent-up inside of me, and I don't know how to release it without getting into trouble.

My only salvation is my girlfriend, Mary. Mary is so pretty and so smart – something I am not. She has such a refreshing naïve outlook on life. She has been raised by a loving and protective family, which contributes to her being such a sweet human being.

Although I admire all these wonderful qualities about Mary, I find myself becoming envious of her and her family. Sometimes I even catch myself resenting them. There have even been times when I have tried to corrupt Mary so she wouldn't be so "perfect", like the time I talked her into drinking when she really didn't want to, and like the time I talked her into having sex before she was ready to have sex. Mary was afraid that I would not respect her anymore if she gave into my demands.

And you know what? She was right.

Oh, I still love Mary. But, I no longer have her up on a pedestal. It makes me feel better about myself if I can keep doing things to corrupt Mary, in order to bring her down to my level.

I am becoming more angry and confused with every passing day. All the reasons I was initially attracted to Mary, all the qualities I loved about her, I now disdain and resent. Now that I have molded her into being more like me, I don't like the person she has become. The fact that she allows me to control her every move has caused me to lose all respect for her.

But, yet, I possess a deep-seated fear of losing her. I don't know what I would do if I ever lost her. I am so afraid of being alone. I don't want to hurt her anymore, but I don't know how to stop. I feel I am in a vicious cycle, like running inside of a wheel in a hamster cage – and I don't know how to jump off.

Mary and I have been married for seven months now. She is about to give birth in three weeks. We both quit school and got married at the courthouse as soon as we found out she was pregnant. I'm working at a local automobile factory – forty plus hours a week – trying to support the both of us.

It is not easy. I'm getting more and more frustrated.

Drinking heavily is no longer enough.

Unbeknownst to Mary, I have now moved on to drugs. Pot, THC, Acid – whatever I can afford at the moment. It depresses me to go home. Since Mary has quit drinking because of the pregnancy, she is insisting I do the same. She wants us to be the "perfect family", but that concept is so severely foreign to my thinking. Therefore, I rarely go home after work. I would rather be out having fun and partying with my buddies – being as loud as I care to be.

It is now only two more weeks before the baby is due. It is 1:15 in the morning as I creep in through the back door, earnestly trying to not wake up Mary. I flip on the kitchen light switch, and there she is, sitting at the kitchen table. Tears are streaming down her face.

"Where have you been?" she cries.

"Out," I answer back, sarcastically. I am so high I can barely stand up.

"I can't go on like this," she softly says. "I won't raise a child this way. I'm leaving you."

"You aren't going anywhere," I boldly reply. I stagger over to the refrigerator and scramble for another beer.

"Danny, I've made up my mind. You're never going to change. I am leaving you."

I violently slam the refrigerator door, rattling all of its contents. Impulsively raising my arm, I rear back and slap her with all my might. I have never done that before. I may have slightly shoved Mary a couple of times in the past, but hit her – NEVER – never before have I hit her.

Mary screams in pain and disbelief. She lays her head on the kitchen table and cries uncontrollably.

I swear I instantaneously sober up.

"Mary, I'm sorry – I'm so sorry! I love you, Mary! Please, forgive me. I'll change, I promise, I'll change.

Please don't cry. Please don't leave!"

There is no consoling her. Overcome by exhaustion, I walk to the bedroom and pass out on the bed.

I wake up the next morning and look at the clock sitting next to the bed. It is 11:23 a.m. Oh, man. I missed another day of work. Why didn't Mary wake me up?

I stumble to the kitchen to use the telephone to call into work. Mary's not in there. I walk past the bathroom. She's not in there. I scramble to the bedroom. Her purse is gone from the top of the dresser. I whip open the closet doors. *Oh my God*, her clothes are missing. I frantically start searching her drawers, the medicine cabinet – gone. All her possessions are gone.

Panic over takes me. *God help me, what am I going to do*? Breathe – breathe deeply.

I dash to the telephone and call Mary's parents. Mary answers the phone. "Mary," I begin to plea with her. "What are you doing? Please come home!"

"It's over, Danny," she answers calmly. "I've made up my mind. I am seeing a lawyer today, and I am getting on with my life. I suggest you do the same thing. Goodbye, Danny."

Silence. She had hung up the telephone.

I begin to tremble erratically. This is it (I rationalize in my mind.) I have nothing left to live for. I never had the love of a father. I lost the love of my mother. I robbed the only person I ever truly loved of the love she once had for me. I love my unborn baby, but will I ever be able to be the kind of father he needs and deserves?

No. I don't think I am capable of that.

I amble back to the bedroom and sit down on the edge of the bed. *Failure.* You are such a failure.

I wanted to be a man. A real man. But I have become a horrible, unlovable beast.

I look at the clock on the nightstand. It's 11:58 a.m. I reach down and open the drawer of the nightstand. I take out the 22-caliber pistol. I place the gun to my temple, tears surging down my cheeks.

This is not how I wanted my life to be.

⌘　　⌘　　⌘　　⌘

My being is soaring and spinning, moving speedily. There is light all around me. The faster I travel, the brighter the light becomes.

I am alone. I see nothing and no one around me. However, the closer I get to the center of the light; I can sense someone is near me. I begin to see a shadow of a figure next to me, so close to me that it appears as if we are molded together, side by side.

"Who are you?"

"Where did you come from?" I ask with my thoughts.

"I am your guide, Altah, and I have always been with you," the answer came.

"Even at your loneliest and darkest moments, I was there. You simply chose not to commune with me; yet, I was always there for you."

Why did I not know someone was there guiding me?

How I wish I had known someone was there with me through this fleeting journey, someone who could have assisted me in sorting out my feelings – someone who could have guided me in evolving into the man I sincerely fervently wanted to become.

I have returned to my true dwelling. I delight in the tranquility, and in the harmony of my siblings. Still, there is an undeniable aching in my spirit.

It is time to join with my counsel, and to share with them my encounters. I express to them how I had carried out the mission that we had laid out. I succeeded in experiencing the path of the male that does not rely on his female alter ego and the light within his spirit. Subsequently, this discovering has left me unfulfilled. The aching I feel in my soul is for a similar journey, but one with some piece of spirituality - some piece of connection.

Yes, we all agree. Another mission is in order. I must continue to experiment further.

Chapter 5

Who Am I – Really?

I begin laying out my plans for a fresh journey.

How does the structure of your created life influence your journey for what is truth? To what degree does your created family influence you in your decision-making to seek the truth? How does your station in life, as well as your geographical position on this plane affect your journey? Or greater yet, how does the irrelevant human-created religious beliefs we are born into script out our plan to define the true meaning of existence?

How concrete is this script of human-created religious beliefs? Can we break free from this script of human-created religious beliefs, or is the family bond of loyalty too suffocating to allow us to break free in search of truth?

If, indeed, this bond of family loyalty and scripted human-created religious beliefs IS too strong to freely break through, can there be any unforeseen circumstances that can assist us in doing so?

I have so many questions and so many anticipations. Although this journey will obtain many frustrations and imprisonments, it is my understanding that it will contain a faceted amount of insight.

I must request extra guidance for this journey. The blockades and struggles I will encounter will be, at times, overwhelming. My council advises me to avoid closing doors, to never stop seeking, and above all, to always be aware of the light within my true self. For it is this true light within me that will be my guide back to home.

The Journey...

I sit here on this ten-foot red padded bench, utterly mesmerized by the animated speaker who is pacing back and forth across the carpeted platform in front of me. My fellow teenage friends, who are sitting next to me, seem to be oblivious to the speaker as they whisper and pass notes back and forth to one another. But I, on the other hand, am enthralled by the words of the speaker. How I wish I was as sure about my spirituality. He is so knowledgeable about the book he teaches from, and he is so positive about what he believes in.

And what a great orator he is. He boldly crescendos at the precise moment. He barely speaks above an audible whisper at the correct time. And then, he gathers all his thoughts into one last resounding climax. Truly, this is a man that is gifted and favored by a source above and beyond our natural resources. He has all the answers to life – his own personal direct line to a higher power. Oh, to be that sure of what you believe in – what is real!

He is a creature of great confidence, and he has every right to be so confident. After all, a higher power chose him, and trusted him, with the secret knowledge and interpretation of universal religious reason.

Tears begin to stream down his cheeks as he lays before us the only two options that are available to us. We can be destined to live forever in a place of utopian beauty, or, we can suffer eternally in a place of damnation.

My heart is pounding so profusely, I fear it will burst out of my chest. I am so utterly afraid. I do not want to go to this evil place of damnation. I know the book from which he teaches, as well as the words he speaks, are infallibly true. My parents have taught me these truths from the time I was born, as their parents have taught them, and their parents before them, and so on.

How grateful I am to have been born in this particular place and time, in order to hear these eternal truths.

However, as immobilized with fear that I am, why am I so hesitant about accepting his great offer to live forever in utopia? Why would anyone in their right mind reject this immaculate gift, knowing the words he speaks are the ultimate and indisputable truth?

Nonetheless, I sit here hesitantly contemplating his offer.

Why?

Is it because, in order to accept his life changing offer I must – as the speaker insists – give up some of my freedoms? Isn't that a miniscule inconvenience compared to the eternal trade off that would be gifted to me?

"Don't be a fool," I tell myself.

I slowly stand up from the red padded bench and hypnotically move toward the front of the auditorium. The speaker thanks me, along with the five other people that have made this life-changing move. We all kneel at the front of the carpeted stage and we all agree in unison to accept the conditions of our commitment.

Several years have passed since that night I joined this organization. I am now a young wife and mother to three small children. I have sat through years of training in the organization. It has taught me to better identify myself, in all aspects of my life, but particularly in my interpretation of my own spirituality. Also, I have passed these teachings on to my children and to other children in the organization, since I became a religious teacher in the organization four years ago.

My life is so organized, so secure. I know where my boundaries are, and it is extremely comfortable living inside these boundaries.

The rules that are laid out for my life free me from worrying about decisions in my life. I don't have to decide what is right or wrong. I don't have to decide who or what to accept – or not to accept. It is all decided for me by the organization, and more importantly, by the organizations interpretation of the book.

Yes, this is a great comfort to me.

At times, as I meditate on my life, I can't help but feel a sadness for people in other parts of this plane. How sad that they haven't had the opportunity I have had to be in a place that teaches me about the absolute truth. I realize there are people trained and destined to travel to other places in order to teach them our truth, but what if they don't reach everyone? What if someone leaves this plane before the truth has been presented to him or her? Then at times I can't help but feel – okay, please forgive me – a sense of superiority.

I must be special. Why would a higher power choose me – insignificant me – to have heard the truth?

Stop! You must stop that evil thought!

After all, the organization teaches us that this kind of thinking is brought on by an evil power that is trying to confuse our thoughts. We must resist this evil power before it consumes our every thought and infiltrates our entire being.

Fighting this evil power can be such an arduous task. It literally drains every bit of my energy. Furthermore, it doesn't seem to be getting any better. It seems the more we fight against the evil, the worse things become. Everyday we see new events and situations arise that we know are evil, and we have to take the time to continuously fight against these events and situations, and/or people, that we know are morally wrong.

What is wrong with this world? Can't this world see that our way is the right way? It is so clear to me; I just don't understand it. This world is becoming such a horrible place; it almost seems as if this evil power is stronger than our higher power.

But I know that simply cannot be true.

My children are now getting older. My oldest daughter, Jessica, is coming into her teen years. She will be attending high school next year, and I dread it with all my might. I don't dread her getting older because her getting older makes *me* feel older, but I dread it because it is getting increasingly more difficult to convince her to follow our belief system. She is beginning to question certain aspects of our beliefs to the point of becoming rebellious at times.

She is starting to question the authority of her father and me. She is starting to listen to music that I know is evil. She has become friends with people whom I believe are evil people. They are evil people because of their strange lifestyles, which go against the teachings of our interpretation of our sacred book. Worst of all, she is even beginning to question portions of the sacred book that our organization is founded upon and holds so dearly – what we believe to be absolute truths.

I don't want to admit it, but there are times when I, too, am confused by the sacred book. There seems to be some portions of the book that I consider being contradictions. We are told we are suppose to be "above it all" and joyous, but on the other hand we are suppose to continuously fight the evil power. How can you be joyous when you are in a constant state of war with an evil power? I have never heard tales of a soldier "laughing it up" out on the battlefield. After all these years, I still haven't figured that part out yet.

I must rid myself of that evil thought, as well. Our leader says we are not to question the book.

The book is infallible, and to question it would be evil.

It is also becoming wearisome, because it seems everyday there is someone, or something, which has crossed over to the evil side that we must fight against. It is becoming more and more difficult to recognize our enemies. More and more people, and situations are now evil – people and situations that used to be acceptable are no longer on our side. Oh well, I suppose that is why our leader refers to us as soldiers. The first job of a soldier is to know who his enemy is.

Jessica just got home from school. She has those two friends with her, again. Matthew, whom I presume, is an all right kid. I just can't seem to get pass his strange hair and all that jewelry in places where it should never be! What kind of mother allows her child to go out of the house looking that way?

Meredith is also with her. I really have a problem with Meredith. The first time I met her I thought she was a boy. Even at her young age, I definitely believe she lives a lifestyle that is very wrong, and goes against the teachings of our organization.

I do try hard to love everyone (and I feel I really do love everyone), but I hate what I see as evil in their lives. I just cannot condone or accept it. If only they would realize that their lifestyles are wrong. It doesn't matter what the world says, if it is against the teachings of the sacred book – *it is wrong!*

The sad thing about it is that they are condemned to spend an eternity in doom, and yet, they refuse to comprehend this fact.

More and more, I find myself in isolation. I am constantly meditating and fighting against the evil power. I am so tired and consumed, but I can't quit. My children's spirits are at stake. I can't quit.

It is five o'clock in the evening. "Jessica," I say, "You need to get ready for our Tuesday meeting at the organization. Your friends are welcome to come along, otherwise they need to leave."

Of course they leave. They think I am some kind of zealot bigot, the poor lost souls. If only they knew the truth.

Six o'clock Wednesday morning we are up as usual. Everyone is in chaos. Bob and the girls are getting ready for work and school. Blake is frantically looking for his homework. I'm making breakfast and packing lunches.

Seven-thirty they are all out of the door. Thank goodness. I can sit down and enjoy my first cup of coffee.

I sit down at the kitchen table with my cup of coffee and sacred book. I open it up and begin to do some reading – but I can't. My mind is too stressed and confused. I just don't have the energy to fight another day.

I begin to let my mind wander off to a peaceful secluded island. Tropical breezes are blowing. No person in sight – just me and the stillness. The only sound I hear is the gentle slap of the waves.

Yes! This is where I want to be today.

Ring! Ring! The sound of the telephone startles me back to reality. It's just as well; I was beginning to feel guilty.

I answer the telephone to find my mother on the other end of the line. For some unknown reason, I begin to confide in her my feelings of confusion and unhappiness.

I soon learn that that was a big mistake. She promptly coerces me into feeling more guilty and selfish. She reminds me that it is not my place to question things – I was not raised that way. She reminds me that what's right is right, and that it is just the evil power trying to get a hold on my thoughts and on me. She hung up with a last, "You know better than that, Gail."

Wow. As I hang up the telephone, I

suddenly feel as if I am twelve years old.

"Is that how I make Jessica feel?" I ask myself.

No, surely not. Ours is a totally different situation. I retrieve my coffee cup from the kitchen table and walk over to the coffeepot to pour myself another cup of coffee. Before I even have a chance to sit down, there is a boisterous knock at the front door.

"What now…?"

I open the door and find myself staring face to face with two city police officers. My heart begins to rapidly palpitate and my mind furiously starts racing.

"Ma'am, would you please come with us – there has been an accident involving your daughter," they calmly speak.

"Oh my God!" I shriek. "Which daughter?"

"Just get what you need, please ma'am, and come with us," they mildly reply.

As we speed down the city streets, I begin frantically throwing questions at the two police officers. Their eerie reserve is making me insane with frenzy.

"Ma'am, we'll be at the hospital in just a moment and they will answer all your questions," they utter at last.

"Do you have a telephone?" I hysterically

blurt out. "I need to call my husband!"

"Ma'am, he has already been notified and is on his way to the hospital."

Why didn't I sense that something horrible was going to happen today? Why didn't I fight the evil force for my daughter this morning, instead of selfishly wandering off to some tropical island? I accused Matthew's mother of being unfit – what kind of a mother *am I?*

Bob is there to meet me as I bolt through the double glass doors of the emergency room. He wraps his arms around me in a confining hold and ceaselessly squeezes his clinch.

"Oh my God, oh my God – what is going on?" My thoughts are panicking.

"It's Jessica," he begins to sob. "She stepped off the school bus and was hit by a car. They don't know if she is going to make it or not."

I limply fall to the floor as if every bone and muscle exited my body in unison. Deliriously, my mind starts screaming at me, "This is not happening, this is not happening!"

Hospital personnel usher Bob and I to a private waiting room. A woman in hospital fatigues begins to unfold the details of our nightmare.

"As Jessica got off the school bus, a car

struck her traveling at a high rate of speed through the school zone. They are preparing her for emergency surgery, but the outcome doesn't look hopeful."

Hopeful? Wait a minute, I thought. My entire existence and spirituality is based on hope. I was always taught that no matter what your circumstances are, there is always hope and healing if you have been faithful and just believe hard enough.

Of course! This is simply a test to see if I really do believe! There is no question about my faithfulness and devotion. Yes, this is just a test!

I begin to feel a diminutive hint of relief. I know I have been questioning some things lately, but deep down I do believe every word in my sacred book. I truly do believe.

The hours of waiting for some confirmation that Jessica is going to be all right is beginning to wear on Bob. As unbearable as the wait is, I have a peculiar ray of peace within me. It is almost as if I have a secret that no one knows about, and I am bursting to tell it to someone, yet, I must keep it to myself.

Bob and I are sitting tightly together, clutching one another's hand, when the surgeon sluggishly enters the waiting room.

"Mr. and Mrs. Talbot?" he asks.

"Yes," Bob frailly answers.

"I'm terribly sorry. I did everything I could – but your daughter didn't make it through the surgery."

A thick black fog immediately and steadily descends, engulfing the entire room. It is as if my total structure is being exterminated. I am utterly and completely numb. There is nothing here. No faith, no hope, no belief system – nothing. I cease to exist.

Where do I go from here?

In a matter of seconds I have gone from believing everything to believing nothing.

⌘   ⌘   ⌘   ⌘

Two hours ago they placed Jessica in the unforgiving cold ground. Bob and I are still sitting here at her gravesite like two zombies. Most everyone has gone home, with the exception of a few of her friends. Mother took Holly and Blake back home with her. Bob and I have no resources to comfort them.

"Mrs. Talbot?" someone whispers grievously.

I gradually lift my head up to see Meredith standing in front of me with tears dripping down her face.

"Mrs. Talbot – I know you never liked me much, but I just want you to know that Jessica was my best friend. She helped me through some very hard times. I know I'm different. I can't help it. But Jessica accepted me for who I am, and she encouraged me to be proud of myself. She taught me to love myself. I will always be grateful to her for that. I just thought you needed to know that."

Meredith slowly walks away to join her nearby friends.

I turn my head to look at Bob. I can tell by the expression on his face that he is having the same thoughts that I am. Jessica had it right all along. We are not here on this plane to judge and to exclude. We are here to help, encourage, include, and to love – to really love. We are to love in a truly unconditional spiritual way, not in a forced religious way.

Maybe, the only evil power that exists is internally. Maybe I have been wasting my time chasing some elusive, external evil power, when all this time – the evil existed in me. Maybe I was the evil one all along, insisting others should look the way I believe they should look, compelling them to live by my standards, my rules and my beliefs.

I look straight ahead at the beautiful varied flowers that are lined around Jessica's gravesite, and I pray – not to some unseen force – but to Jessica.

"Jessica, I know you can hear me, because I can feel you all around me. Thank you for the lesson, baby girl. I love you, always."

Chapter 6

Viability

As I prepare to ascend to my new homeland, I groom my psyche for the trip we are embarking upon. I begin breaking free from all the liberties we share, and all the joy we establish. I begin breaking free from my male/female counterparts and solitarily drift onward with only my force as my guide.

The Journey...

Again I awake on this plane. My soul is becoming tired. Agonizing journeys seem to deplete ones spirit. I know my mother must wonder why she ever gave birth to me in the first place. I am not very easily satisfied. I thirst for more – trying to rush this journey along.

Patience is not a strong suit of mine.

On this trip I notice differences in myself. I feel as if I stand outside the distant crowd, looking in. Even as I play with the other children, I seem to be projected away from them, as if I am watching a movie of sorts – in which I am the star. The other children seem to treat me differently. Oddly, I don't believe they even know the reason why they treat me so differently.

As I grow, I find myself more and more perplexed. I'm quite aware of the fact that I am a boy in my outside physical appearance, but in my heart I enjoy the same wonders as my female counterparts. Is this wrong? It seems to be conflicting and unconventional.

I wonder what it is, and what will become of it.

I am afraid of the contrast that lives in this

body. It is becoming increasingly more difficult to deal with the opposition, the older I progress.

Settling into my teen years, I have become a loner. I feel a connection with no one. These are very sad and desolate times for me.

My school peers tease me and call me a sissy. No one seems to understand me. I don't understand me. I know my mother loves me, But at times I feel she has a sense of fear about me. There are some things I simply can't talk to her about. My father left my mother a few years ago, and we haven't heard from him since then. I really don't care that he left. Like my school peers, he never really liked me either.

I hate all my schoolteachers. I actually think they are all from another world in outer space!

Walking into the front doors of my school, Josh Anderson, one of the buffoons who plays football, rams me from behind. In passing he says, "Get out of my way punk, you remind me of my retarded sister."

I say nothing while thinking sarcastically to myself, "Why thank you, have a great day. Bye-bye."

Collecting myself, I head down the hall again. Doing so, I feel an arm slip around my shoulder.

A tender voice says, "Are you all right?"

I look up to see a sweet smile from a young lady, probably around twenty-two years old, or so. I have never seen her before, but immediately I feel a connection to her.

She continues, "People like that have no manners. He'll get his one day."

Then off she went down the hall, filtering in with the hundreds of students.

"Who was that?" I thought. "Was she a teacher?"

That was the first time a superior ever spoke to me as if I was human. She actually touched me and connected with me in a positive way. What a refreshing contrast to the earlier connection I had with Josh Anderson!

I begin walking a little taller this morning, careful still not to make eye contact with anyone.

Getting to my first period class and waiting for the bell to ring, I stare straight ahead. I don't want to look at anyone. I don't want to give someone the opportunity to pounce on me.

I notice out of the corner of my eye the teacher entering the classroom. It is not our regular teacher.

As she came into full view, I could see it is

the woman who spoke to me in the hall. Mesmerized, I can't take my eyes off her. She looks directly at me and says, "Well, hello again."

My face turns red and I muster a blubbered, "Hello."

Everyone in the entire classroom turn his or her head to look at me. I feel my hands start to sweat as I grasp the desk and begin to melt into the chair. As the attention focuses back on the teacher, she announces that she is taking over the class for Mrs. Riggs, our former English teacher.

My spirit rises the more she speaks. For the first time in my life I feel a connection with another human being. The loneliness, the humiliation of being different, is beginning to dissipate. For an instant I feel as if I am a whole being.

I begin spending afternoons with Janice Taylor, the new English teacher. She awakes in me a need to discover who I am and where I am going.

Don't get me wrong, high school is still extremely difficult.

However, my meetings with Janice have turned me around from having a feeling of suicide, to having a new feeling of fresh hope.

She tells me there are similar people in the world that feel the same way as I feel. She says the reason she knows is because she is one of them. It isn't just a need to find love with a person of the same sex, but a need to interpret the emptiness inside of me and to fill this void that I have carried around all my life.

She explains that other people's prejudices against her and me are created out of their own fears, fear of the unknown, and fear of something different.

My life is becoming so much more full, since that first day I met Janice Taylor. Janice and I continue to keep in contact. My dreams and expectations of this life have opened up and have found a place in my once sad soul. I have opened my heart and mind, not to the difficulties that cripple my existence, but to the possibilities of living – living fully – unabashed and liberated.

Who would have thought this scrawny little boy could have come full circle? Who would have thought that? Certainly not me!

I still maintain my ups and downs. There are some things I would like to change – some things I would not. Merely, the same as anyone else, I suppose. I really only want to love and be loved. Like a bird in a cage, I long for the freedom to be – to be just me.

⌘　　⌘　　⌘　　⌘

Now I lie here on this bed of death, waiting for my exit papers. I never would have dreamed I would contract such a disease. What a joke this is.

Touché to all those people that despised me.

I have a few remaining friends, including my precious Janice, who still remains a good friend. I bestow to her one half of my worldly possessions, which have accumulated to quite a lot over the years. My friends have called all my relatives, but none seem to care enough to come for a visit.

Imagine that.

I have not spoken to my family in years; not even during my time of need will they put down their shields of hatred for a chance to mend a dying relationship (pardon the pun on words). Well, no need for regrets. Nothing can be changed now. Maybe someday they will understand my ways or, maybe not.

This room seems very dark. I wish someone would pull the curtains back. I think I hear someone coming. No, maybe not. I see a small light trying to slip through the curtain. It is becoming brighter. The curtains are being pulled apart while the light engulfs them, encircling the room around me as it swallows the stillness that surrounds me.

I suddenly feel the wholeness that evaded me most of my life. Was it always here? Did I allow this plane to consume myself - consume my soul?

To feel the pain that people had bestowed on me, I must have unknowingly allowed their pain and ignorance to be incorporated into my composition. I thought my feelings were made of iron, impenetrable as a door of steel.

I guess the joke is on me.

I sense all these perceptions wash from my soul. What I understand now as I leave this bourgeois of mental emotions, what is lasting and what is remaining, is this small piece inside of me – this minute structure of substance which took a lifetime to live, which fits on the tip of my finger. From all of this that is left, the long days and nights, the pain and the agony, the sweat and staleness, the good and the worthless, this small light of love transcends me back home.

Home, to where I belong – home, to where I am expected, longingly rewarded by the firmament of true reality.

Be patient, be kind. Embrace your brothers and sisters, embrace their love and embrace their differences.

Accept the unacceptable. Bring them home again.

Here I leave behind the negativity of this neighboring homeland. Now I pick up my state of existence I have longed for unknowingly, the realm of certainty. The challenge is complete. I proceed home with the feeling of accomplishment, opening up again to my world of dreams.

Beautiful serenity – take me home.

I realize how far I have come on this voyage; somewhat resulting from the dolorous situations I found my psyche to be under. Alas, another piece of the pie. I am growing outwardly and inwardly, finding vision in the dark masses that hold the secrets of life on this plane, nonetheless, being wholly aware of the differences in nature and diverseness of beings. Albeit, the one true connection of viability is the unseen veins that stem as in the root of a tree.

This viability is the driving force that connects each and every one of us here. It connects us to the in-between, making life on the plane, not really here, but everywhere.

Unforeseen is the existence related, yet not related, with all sides emerging as a victor.

Man has decided what is dark and what is light. In the name of beliefs, we have chosen what is wrong and what is right, causing a vibration affect into the outer senses. Then, we make laws from the cause and effect, not realizing everyone cannot fit into those guidelines. Instead of accepting people and their possibilities, we drive people into seclusion, categorizing people into a realm of negative behavior. We set them up for destruction. We cause them to believe that if they do not fit here, they must not fit anywhere.

The attitude of man shudders this mind. I am glad to leave behind these shadows, but in the same sense I am bereaved for my siblings which I leave behind a tangled world that is searching for stability, a world that is lost without a form of compassion.

All of this, I leave behind.

Chapter 7

The Pain Of Hope

As I stand here ready for departure, the length of the transformation overwhelms my spirit. I feel the endurance and pain being delivered to every ounce of my being. The sadness engulfs my senses. A tremendous amount of suffering is my gift to this plane.

Will my soul adhere to the promise of love?

Will I prosper in the belief of knowing the will of being?

My destination is unknown. Faith is guiding my every step, even with the unbelievable amount of misery.

I relish in this journey, the journeys of tomorrow and the journeys of yesterday, henceforth, creating a visual of life expectancies. I revel in the knowledge of the undiscovered; creating this life of mysteries joined with the power of my god-force and guides. A vanishing awareness of hyperactivity embellishes my inner spirit. This small gust of wind will drive me the distance, amorously delivering the steady force of power and protection all the days of this animated adventure.

Reflection will be the tool I use to return. I take in hand the hope and aspirations of rejoining with my kindred spirits.

I place my hands against the glass of tomorrow's visions. I watch this new life play out in front of me. The illumination of this dream is staging its' way in the foreground and is growing into my reality, casting down the enveloped structure of the final product. There is not one, but many intertwined ideals and expectations – not always knowing where one is going or where one will end up. Regardless – taking home with me the few samples of memories when I leave. Gifts from this adventure are never what one would imagine, but they are sometimes what one would try to forget.

Reveling in this moment and savoring every detail of this experience ensures the richness of the adventure – arriving full and ready for the journey.

I set my wings to flight. Lift me up and let me fly!

Through the glass I filter, uniting with the life I am to become for now and forever. Beholding this experience as a benefit to my soul, I leave no need to return. I go by way of certainty and reliance. Let no individual disrupt the mission that is in place!

I must keep my feet on my path and delight in all my endurances.

The Journey...

My first few years are hazy. I have all this knowledge filtering in my head, but yet, I cannot speak. I feel my guide interpreting. I am cold and hungry, and I long for love.

I am five years old (in these years), and my memory seems to have faded into a dream. It is just a dream, along with all the volumes and volumes of other dreams. I laugh, I love, I cry. This is what I can share with you now – only this. For my ride into the unknown has officially begun.

I fought my way through my early years, grabbing at every chance of happiness I could find – which was far and few between. My memories clouded heavier with each passing year, until I find myself always inside looking out. I recognize my existence as being familiar, yet, I feel misplaced and bitter. I feel as if I only have myself to rely on, especially since the people in authority don't seem to know anymore than I do. However, they will shake their irritating fingers in my face, as if they did. I am becoming more confused as the years roll by.

My life is so terrifying. I hate everything and

everybody. I hate our apartment building. I hate our small apartment. I especially hate my mother for allowing us to be in this place. I just had my tenth birthday, with no great celebration. The fourteen-year-old boy down the hall keeps pulling me under the stairs, grabbing at all my privates. I hate him. The man upstairs says I don't deserve to live, because of the color of my skin. I don't know why he hates me so, but I hate him, too.

My mother is out of her head most of the time, on drugs or drinking, I really can't tell which one anymore. What is the difference, anyway? She whips me for being like her and she whips me for not being like her. I cry to myself in the night when I am alone, or, I am almost alone – I knock a roach bug from off my leg.

No one hears my sobs.

I cry, "I want to go home."

But, I don't know where home is.

All I know is that I long for it. I dream of it. My dreams are the only rescue I have. I go there every night when I am alone.

In my dreams I can be like the family on television.

The family has a beautiful white house with the tiny white fence running all the way around the house. They have the cute little shaggy dog that runs out to say "hello" whenever I get home from school. I, then, walk up the path to the front door where my mother is waiting to open the door for me – *just for me!*

I can smell the cookies baking in the kitchen oven. My daddy wants me to come and sit on his lap, so that I can tell him about my day. He reads me a story from any book that I want him to, because I have so many books to choose from. Hundreds and hundreds of them! Then, both my parents tuck me into bed at night. We say our prayers and then I say, "Goodnight, mommy. Goodnight, daddy. I love you both so very much!"

But sadly they disappear.

All I can smell is the stink coming from that dang toilet that doesn't flush half of the time. The apartment is too quiet, except for that mouse that comes out every night at this time. It is 3 o'clock in the morning and my mom should be home by now.

I'm scared.

"Shh - shh - shh - go back to sleep. Don't think about it," I try to tell myself.

I feel the tears burning my eyes. I want to die. Please, just let me die. Maybe I will get a new family, one that loves me and that I can love back. Maybe that kitty cat will be in the alley behind our building, again, tomorrow.

Oh, I hope so!

I wake up early the next morning and walk into the kitchen. There is mom, lying on the living room floor. There is some strange man stretched out on the couch. I have never seen him before. I get a piece of stale bread out of the cupboard. It looks like our little mouse got his breakfast out of it first. I grab it and run quietly out the door – ever so quietly. I don't want to wake up that stupid kid down the hall, and I certainly don't want to wake up that ugly man upstairs.

I run as fast as I can, around to the back of our building. Beside the big green dumpster I squat down in the corner to pee, being very careful not to get it in my shoes. I hear some voices! I stay crouched down here in the corner until they go away.

I begin looking for the kitty. I thought he might have stayed the night in the dumpster, but he is not in there. Where, oh where, can he be? Then I see him – stretched out between two cement blocks. Blood is coming out of the top of his head and out of his mouth. Someone must have hurt him. I feel his body. Ice cold. "Why would someone do this to a poor little kitty cat?" I yell.

Tears begin running from my eyes. The ache and longing came back from the night before. Why didn't you take me with you, kitty? *Why?!*

I would have gone with you.

I close my eyes and hold his tiny paw in my hand. I dream of us playing in the alley. He is chasing me, trying to catch my dirty shoestring. I laugh so hard! I hold him and feel his cold nose against mine. We would have had some good times, Mr. Kitty. I lay him back between the two cement blocks and walk away. Far away.

YES! Far, far away! The words keep screaming through my head. I start running and running, until I can't breathe anymore – then I run some more. I do not want to breathe. YES! To breathe no more! This is my secret wish. It is my only wish.

Now, all I have to do is wait, for I know that wishes do come true. I stumble around the alleys for a couple of days, sleeping wherever I can find a soft spot, not knowing where I am or even who I am.

It is getting dark again. I need to find somewhere to sleep. I am feeling so much clearer than I have ever felt. I even smile, as I look at my skinned up knees. A feeling of relief comes over me.

I head down the alley and I cross the street. I suddenly have a feeling of warmth encircling me – like a blanket that has been warmed and tucked tightly all around me - keeping out all the cold.

I feel confused, but not afraid. Curious, I guess is the word. I am floating – I think. It feels as if I am floating!

As I look down, I can see myself lying on the ground, wrapped in a blanket inches away from a car. I am not moving. I am not moving, at all. Who are all those people? I don't know them – not one of them. I then hear a voice. Where is it coming from? I turn around. As I turn around, a glorious bright light encompasses my eyes. All I can see is light – light in every angle and love.

I feel love!

The more I feel it, the more I want it. This is it! I remember, now. *This* is my wish! This is what I had wished for. Wishes *do* come true!

Hurling toward the light, the life I know I am leaving behind is floating by me and encircling me, portions of a life I have forgotten – or wanted to forget. These pieces of my life are playing around and around in circles, encompassing my head. It reminds me of something unclear. I don't care, though. I am happy. Happy in this dream.

No more pain. My knees don't hurt anymore. The longing in my heart is going away. Strangely, the life I'm leaving behind does not seem to haunt me. More amazingly, I think it is actually helping me, helping to guide my way. With arms outstretched, I am flying!

Me – little me! Flying!

I feel larger than life – when unexpectedly I hear a faint cry. I have to see where the sound is coming from. I feel as if I am being pulled backwards.

"*No!* I don't want to go back!"

I scream within, "Please – please, no!"

As I sail reluctantly back, I hear a voice that says, "I am with you – we are all with you."

I awake to a clamoring of metal, and an aroma of a gas that has a funny taste and bloats my stomach.

Where am I?

It is all white and silver. I am in some sort of a mental fog. I can scarcely see people moving about; nor can I make out their faces.

I know I will be in big trouble. They will probably put me in jail! But I don't care. I do not want to go back. I never want to see my mother again. I fall back asleep, my only escape.

When I awake, again, I can see much more clearly. I look around. I am in a very big bed. The room is very large, much larger than my bedroom in my small apartment. I am the only one in the room. Is it a hospital? Or, is it a prison hospital like my mom and her friends talk about? I can feel my tears flowing, burning my cheeks. What am I to do? What is going to happen to me? I'm scared, so very scared. Help me – please, someone help me.

I sob into the clean white sheet, worrying the entire time that I will get into trouble for soiling "their" clean white sheet.

I hear someone entering my room. I try to see who she is through my tears. She is speaking to me, but I can't quite understand. She is now sitting next to me on the bed, patting my shoulder ever so gently.

"Hush, baby," she says. "Please don't cry. I'm here with you, and I am not going to leave you."

I look up at her – into those beautiful dark eyes. She is an angel all dressed in white. The light that shines through those dark eyes seems to be able to see inside of me, as if she knows me and knows everything I have been through. If only I had known, I would have wished for her!

How my life has changed from that day on. I am staying with that beautiful angel, Sondra, and her husband, John. They adopted me sometime after I found out my mother and her man friend had been murdered the day I ran away from home. I believe the day I was given wings, I was being prepared for my deliverance from the dangers that were fast approaching. Sondra babies me, and she never forgets to tell me that she loves me. She loves everything about me.

I try to never look back. But, sometimes that is hard to do – very hard to do.

John is strong and he gives me short, tight hugs. I can tell he doesn't want to make me feel uncomfortable by his closeness. I know he loves me, too.

⌘   ⌘   ⌘   ⌘

Sondra and John both lived long and healthy lives. I miss them both dearly.

This morning, as I sit here on my 87th birthday, I feel clearer than I have in quite some time. I even smile as I look down at my old wrinkled knees – where the scabs used to be – and a feeling of perfect relief comes over me.

Chapter 8

A Glimmer Of Home

All the love I left behind comes flooding into my being, as I return into our atmosphere. The coolness sweeps my existence and fills me to the highest state.

Whatever I left behind on that plane, feels as though it was something imagined. Was it imagined? Or, is my memory being taken away and the entire harm is being erased – leaving behind only the motive?

I welcome my counterparts, whom I had a strong affinity for in the new plane – and here at home.

I was home, again.

The love that saturates me incites me to feel whole again. The love was always with me, but I feel it was just slightly out of reach, barely a scarce recollection. How could something so superior feel as though it was left behind? I want to discuss this with my guide.

Now it is time to sit with my elders and blend our minds and spirits. As they arrive I embrace each one of them, collectively and individually. I have truly missed them. Of course, they have not missed me – since they were always there with me. Contrastively, I just have a very minute recollection of their presence with me in the new plane. Nonetheless, I am so happy to be back in their presence. I am thrilled to be able to share with them my many experiences while in the new plane.

Feeling a meager part of me is still mortal; I express to my elders my desire to go back to this plane so that I may be with my mother – who is still completing her mission in the new plane. Everyone agreed with my wish and went about to make it possible.

While I am preparing for my next voyage, I relish being home. The peace and serenity is insurmountable. To attempt to put into words the contentment and utopia that inundates my being would be futile. My hope for this journey is that I can remember *this moment* when I am in the other world. I sense it might be easily accomplished on this next voyage. I am very exhilarated and at peace regarding this new voyage and the prospect of being with my mother's spirit on this fresh obscure habitation.

The Journey...

As I awake on this new plane, I begin to feel bright lights accompanied with a burning sensation in the pit of my stomach. It is as if I am being pulled from my mother. I have a strange awareness, as if I have arrived too early for my mother. Consequently, I am becoming very distressed. Something is amiss.

My first recollection of this new day is of someone announcing ecstatically, "It's a boy!"

Diversely, I do not feel the same type of joy as I do on some of my other journeys. My mother is not holding me. In fact, I have no idea where my mother is, or if she is even near me.

The reason I came back so soon was to see my mother, and now, I am alone and I cannot even feel her essence. I am saddened. *Please, don't make me stay here if I cannot be with my mother.*

Lights begin flashing! Bells begin ringing loudly! Someone is beating on my chest while someone else is shoving a tube down my throat. People are sticking needles in me at every angle. *Oh father, please help me! Take me back home – oh please, oh please.* I begin to feel lifeless – no pain. I am falling into sleep. I hear someone cry out.

Mother? Mother? Is that my mother?!

Tears fall.

I awake to find something heavy sheltering my eyes.

I can't see! I'm hurting all over. I can't seem to move, and I don't feel as if I am capable of moving. The sounds are loud and strange, like the clanging of metal. I can hear people talking, but I do not denote any feeling of emotion in their voices. I cannot detect whether they are happy or sad. I wish I had a clue as to what is going on around me.

I decide to cry out!

I scream with all the determination I can muster – nothing. I try again – nothing – not so much as a murmur. I'm frightened and I'm crying, and yet, no one seems to be aware of it. The only explanation my soul can deduce is that the tube in my throat, somehow, must be blocking my sound waves.

I just decide to drift back into sleep and dream. I dream a lovely dream of my mother. She is dressed all in white. Her skin looks so rosy and her arms are outstretched waiting – waiting for me.

I awake once again, and once again

someone is beating on my chest. They are now flipping me over and doing the same procedure on my back. Subsequently, someone begins shoving another tube down my throat.

What are they doing?!

I decide to try and scream, again, when I begin to feel a warm sensation in my stomach. It starts to fill me. I feel the first evidence of some contentment since I started this excursion. Once again, I decide to slip off into sleep.

I can see her in my dreams. It must mean she is close – if not in this world – then back home. But, wait. If she still remains in this world, why am I left alone with strange people that I do not feel an affinity towards? If she hasn't yet arrived, I hope she will soon, before the loneliness overpowers me and I lose the will to want to stay on this plane. Or worse, I will begin to lose my memories of home and I will not be able to recognize the one true light that shines through my eyes.

There is not much time, since my voyage here is to be brief. *Mommy, please come quickly.* The pain and the aggravation are so intense. I do not know how long I will hold out!

Again I awake, wondering how long I have

been in this place, maybe a day in this world's time? The sounds are so magnified! They send waves of phenomenal pain from the top of my head, to the bottom of my feet. The sadness I feel is swallowing me deeper and deeper into a blackness – a place, where I do not want to go. The pain and agony are destroying me.

The people that are assisting me do so with very little emotion. It's as if I am nothing, just something they have to contend with at the moment. I do not know how long I can hold on. The little fight that is left in me is rapidly dissipating. Again, I drift back to sleep.

My dreams are so vivid. I get glimpses of home and family. My attachments there seem to be pulling me back. I wonder if it is my family pulling the strings, or is it my yearning to leave this concourse of torture?

It doesn't matter.

It seems as though I will never see the only one I came to seek out. I can't even leave this place in quiet dignity. With the constant beating on my chest, I have no way of stopping the very thing that is keeping me alive. Peace…peace – come simply to me. Let me forge on with honor and glory.

I lay still watching the light change from behind my shielded eyes, going from dark to light. I hear voices coming. It sounds like they are wheeling in another machine.

Please, no more machines! Just let me be.

The sounds are getting louder as they near my room. They must be bringing in more babies that are in the same shape as I am, no doubt. I transmit my heart and spirit out to them to comfort and console them. But I am wrong; it is not more children. The voices I hear are near. I feel a strong vibration in the pit of my soul! My spirit is uniting with someone so close. Are they in a bed? I listen carefully with all my senses alive.

Oh, my – is it? Can it be?

She lives!

The only reaction I can establish is to wail and thrash my arms about violently. Someone tries to calm me, but to no avail. At this moment I feel her presence. Her human hand slips over mine and I feel the warmth of her spirit engulf my spirit. I silence myself and listen fervently. I praise the day I entered this galaxy! I praise the day they "tortured" me to keep this body alive! The pain, the agony, the sorrow – for all of this – to feel her touch and to know she lives I would do this a thousand times over.

No regret will ever come from me – not ever.

I lay ever so still listening to her voice. She is cooing and calling me by name – my given name on this plane. I can tell by her tone that she has no recollection of who we are or where we have come from, which is more than natural. The calmness I feel within this self is lustrous. I will value every moment that I am in this state. I will allow no man to regret the day they set eyes upon me. Without uttering a word, this tiniest of being will be an example of love and understanding. I received the greatest gift of all, and my gift was granted so early. This very moment shall live greatly in the heart of my soul forever and ever.

The visit I had with my mother that day was all too brief. I sensed she, too, was in some pain, probably caused by the birthing experience. It has been a few months since that experience. I have opened the door to passing over on several occasions – which has been brutally discomforting to my mother. It is oppressive to see her grieve so. Her remembrance of who we really are is lying deep within herself, but she can neither see it with her eyes nor touch it with her hand.

Someday it will come to her. Perhaps it will come as a small sequence of dreams, or maybe, all at once – like a thought or a visual.

But for now, the pain and agony are her path. It is all she can hold onto because her faith only creeps in small intervals.

I enjoy every moment we share together. She is permitted to hold me now as she rocks me off to dreamland – dreamland, where I visualize better days and a healthy exterior. Still and all, in reality, this body grows weaker and my spirit is pulling me home. I feel it a great honor to have lived this short life. The anguish was worth the momentary time I spent with her in the natural state of motherhood.

She is standing beside my bed gazing into my eyes. Our eyes are the same – as if looking into a mirror. We see deeply past the surface of the eyes and we concentrate on blending our souls. This short time we have shared together will give her strength and abilities unknown to her now.

My time has come. I feel as if I am being pulled away. I can hear my mother crying. She is telling my caregiver to change my tube and she is reminding him of the last time I slipped into unconsciousness. No one seems to be listening to her. Her cries are haunting.

⌘　　⌘　　⌘　　⌘

I am drifting.

I find myself in a small room watching my mother hold my lifeless vessel. She is alone. She rocks back and forth holding my body against hers. The sobbing and pleading seem to be restraining me. She unsuccessfully breathes into my mouth in an attempt to revive me. I hope I am leaving behind some abundance of the love I shared and will always share with her. Her "failures" on this plane are of no consequence to me. I only know of the things we retain from these ventures. The things we have contributed to each other – love, kindness, growth. These things can never be placed in mere words.

As I navigate myself home, I know there is a piece of my soul that I have left behind – which my "forever mother" can look back on and remember each day that I was a member of this plane. Another piece is left behind so she can see glimpses of whom we truly were and who we are to become, for I will forever ride with her through the life I left behind – until we meet again.

My heart is with you, mother. Thank you for giving me this time to share with you.

You will remember me, in time.
I will remember this time, forever.

Chapter 9

Authentic Spiritual Awareness

The Journey...

Anew day has dawn. I feel very connected to my mother head, who has me strapped to her back. I know my memory should be failing me; however I feel so complete, just as I did in my homeland. My vibrations run abundantly deep.

I have an intimacy with the grass beneath my feet, with the stars that illuminate above my head, and with the wind and the air I breathe. I feel a oneness; I feel a circle of awareness that cannot be severed.

My mother works endlessly and she is well regarded by all her tribesmen. I believe her to be some breed of medicine woman. The bundles she carries are sacred, somehow protecting our people's health, as well as all forms of life. Finding the offending predator, my mother mends our people outwardly from the spirit. She has the capability to communicate with all spirits; to find the individuality of each soul; to answer all their wants and needs.

We are a strong people that can run faster than the wind. We can feel warmth in the freezing temperatures. Our good health rarely fails us.

I would say I am very close to home. There is a very fine line between the voyage on this new plane and with my home. There is a spiritual awareness that runs through our blood like crystal clear waters. Visions of wisdom and of life come to us, generously and effortlessly, even in my tiny mind.

As the months begin to pass and as I grow into my first years, my visions of my homeland do not diminish. I expect I will carry these shadows of my home with me, however long the number of days I travel on this plane – on this voyage. I cannot seem to be able to separate the two; they seem to be as one.

With arms outstretched, I can lie in the fields of grass, gazing at the sky, while visions whirl through my head. The grass beneath my back becomes a part of me, filtering through my loins. I can feel the energy pumping inside of me while cleansing my soul. Clutching the greenery and the soil beneath my fingernails, we become whole. The air filters through the trees, the grass, the clouds and me. I sense the blood, the heart, the rotation of the cycle, delivering my spirit into a suspended array of enlightenment.

Overcome by joy, I awaken and walk on a new path this day. The visions of this life – and the next life – run swiftly through my mind.

As I continue to grow into a young brave, I envision a life unknown to me. It is a life that is changing and growing increasingly uncertain.

I am perplexed by a recurring vision. A dream? Perhaps – yet, I am awake. I look out over the tranquility of the horizon. The sky is intensely blue with the spattering of billowy clouds suspended in mid air. I see a dense powder of dust that is rapidly enlarging as it draws near. Emerging from these dry particles of traveling land are two magnificent, untouched stallions, racing toward where I am standing. One mount is as white as the snow in early morning. The other great steed is as black as a cloudy, starless night. As I stand here in my native-born land, facing the two colossal mammoths that are simultaneously racing at the speed of wind, I wonder at their strength and beauty. As they appear in full view, I speculate if they will halt, or, if they will pass directly through me – as if I weren't even here. My pondering lasts but only a few more moments – for before my eyes in the small distance the two marvelous stallions suspend their flight towards me. They each turn in unison to face their opponent. Uniformly, they rear up on their hind legs and begin to battle with their massive fore legs. Their hoofs appear to clamor consistently with each other; yet, there is no sound – no winner and no loser.

The vision ends just as suddenly as it begins – only to surprisingly replay itself, again and again. Nothing is changing; the exact same occurrences take place, step by step.

My spirit fights to try and explain the message of the vision. I feel as if something is missing, something close at hand that I cannot quite grasp in my hand. My senses are strong, but for the first time in this life I feel fear hovering around my existence.

Years go by and I find myself becoming a strong soul, but the fears I have still haunt me from time to time. I have a powerful mate who matches both my strengths and love. She blends well with her surroundings, just as the deer that hide in the forest. One moment they are there and the next moment they are gone, the unseen – masquerading as a tree, a branch, or a blade of grass – hidden from the eye, but remaining for the senses.

Today we have tales from afar. There are a people who have invaded our territory. Their skin is pale – fearfully pale – and unnatural. They are starving for food, incapable to care for themselves! Our brothers and sisters have fed and nourished the bodies of the strange people, as well as provided them with shelter. We heard that these people arrived in very large vessels, which I hope they return in, since news of these people frightens me.

Don't they have a home – a home of their own? I don't understand "a man without a homeland". How can that be?

If they won't leave, maybe our brothers and sisters can help them to understand our way of life. Maybe they can teach them to be as one with the land – to give back to the land what the land gives to us. Yes, I am sure these strangers will bestow the same tidings to my siblings, as they did to them. I am sure these strangers will not cause harm to our land, nor to the inhabitants that have wandered here for thousands of years. Certainly all people have the same knowledge of the land, knowing it is a borrowed treasure.

Don't all people share the same beliefs – the same ideals?

I stop to think of our peaceful home. In our home, we drift through the vastness of it's' fields, and we share and care for what is borrowed. We give back to the land when we lay this carcass into the ground, again and again, as our many fathers and mothers did before us.

My vision keeps plaguing my thoughts with fears, but my heart tells me these people are also my brothers and sisters. Would you cause your siblings and their families harm? Would you go into their homes and be discourteous with their environment? No, this cannot be.

A cold stillness submerges my being, but I fervently tell myself all will be well. All our blood comes from the one spirit father. We must all share some common ideals of our homeland – ideals of protection, of honor, or repayment.

Still, I cannot dismiss the coolness in my blood today.

As I gaze out over the land, I see many horses with riders approaching. From a distance, the riders clothing appear unusual. As they come nearer I can see the paleness of their skin.

And still they come.

⌘ ⌘ ⌘ ⌘

My time has ended on the new plane. What I had feared certainly did come to pass. Did I cause this affliction through my fear? I will consult my makers.

As I soar home, my arms are being uplifted with the help of my guides. We are moving swiftly through bright white clouds, each arm connected and intertwined.

On my right is my guide on this new plane, my brother flowing through my sister, the eagle. Each one is simultaneously trading forms – which shows me the love and connection we each share. One cannot be without the other. This time and moment is the strongest fulfillment these four souls can share.

As I look into the face of the eagle, his eyes shine with a brilliance of light that transpires energy and love. We communicate through our minds and spirits. As my heart is still banded to the life I was leaving behind, I want to know why our land was being overcome with beings who are destroying the land and the inhabitants, thus throwing off the balance of the plane.

My eagle guide then shows me (through his

eyes) the ignorance and fear of these beings that once had the ability to make this land become as great as what we share here at home. However, it will now take a much longer journey. A journey that will bring destruction. A journey that will darken the waters and spoil the land. Then, after they realize what they have done – an even longer journey attempting to erase the damage that they created.

The circle. The circle of life. The circle of creation. The circle of time. Taking the long road home, because of hatred and the need to control. *The purpose is denial.*

Out of their fabricated religions that begin with love, but lose their way in the darkness of fear, they believe they have the right to kill their brothers and devastate their domain. In the name of their god, they came, they pillaged, and they conquered – in the name of love. In the name of our brother, they run in a labyrinth. They forgot why we are on this journey. The sadness spreads across the land, trying to redeem this great tragedy, trying to rectify the humiliation and disturbance.

The great eagle, my brother/my sister, draws me nearer to home. The slights that were made seem to be slipping away, sucking out of my being and allowing me to fulfill this circle of moments. I realize that even in non-enlightenment comes a spark of light – like that of my brother the eagle. Through his eyes and guidance comes a brilliance of knowledge that relaxes my soul and allows me to realize these beings that were sent to that plane, will one day come into full circle. They can destroy the body, but they can never destroy the soul. For I will return and try to purify what has been incurred, just as my brother has come in many forms – not always recognized by the eye – but always made light unfold upon a dark day.

As I walk through my homeland, my sense of peace returns to me. I carry a warm glow in me for the time I have spent away. I rejoice in my return.

Maybe next time I will not allow fear to be my ruler. I will decide when the time comes. My hunting ground is now peaceful again. I lie on the unfurrowed land; surrounded by all creatures great and small, heralded by all spirits who revel in the knowledge that all life – wherever it may wonder – is all well and good. From the great eagle, to the fairies that tend to the unprotected, we will all see you on the next plane.

Chapter 10

Soul Connected

Despite the feeling of total fulfillment that my homeland offers me, I incessantly have a beckoning need to take off on yet another journey – a final journey – or a soon to be final journey.

I have a persistent desire to explore, in depth, the male/female separation of qualities, and to uncover the mysteries of the incorporation of these two diverse entities.

As this will begin the ending stages of my journeys on that plane, I wish this journey to be an almost complete fruition. Since I am indeed entering the final chapters of my journeys on the new plane, I long for this upcoming voyage to closely resemble the union I have with my fellow siblings here at home.

Once again, I confer with counsel as to my

plans and preparation. Not surprising, they were already in agreement and were already creating groundwork for my exploration before our gathering took place.

I immerse myself in an extra dose of love and energy. The impulses are so mighty within my siblings and me; the experience almost causes me to squelch my deep passion for another journey. Still, I know this is a mission I cannot abort. I know this is a mission that will unfold secrets and desires, a mission that will tap into the most vehement of emotions.

The Journey...

Swiftly running above the shoreline, over the mounds of kelly green grass, rocks, wildflowers and yellow St. John's Wort, it is quickly becoming nightfall.

I didn't mean to be this late. I am always there long before dusk. Every evening I climb out onto the abundant black rocks and am firmly seated in ample time to face and watch the majestic sunset fall behind the glorious gray highlands.

Why did my chores take so long today? "I need to gain speed," I think as I pick up the bottom of my long pleated wool skirt. "If only I could wear trousers as men do, I could run much faster."

The sun is now being swallowed up in the narrow horizon between the two far off mountains, as I finally find my familiar place on the edge of the black rocks. I lift my long wool skirt and sit cross-leg, facing the falling sun. The last of the rays from my old friend, the sun, are glistening across the sea – reaching out to welcome me – to tell me goodnight before he would close another door on another day.

The protective highlands will now keep me sheltered as I alternate my gaze between the empty horizon in front of me, and the thousands of stars above me – as I do every evening.

As I briefly and gently close my eyes, I can hear the far off sound of crying bagpipes in the back of my mind. Then – the face of my beloved sailor appears to me.

I can envision every contour of his face – his square jaw, his impish smile – but in particular, his eyes. His dark, yet, delicate eyes – that connects our souls. It is his eyes that speak to me and let me know that all that matters in this vast universe is our love, no matter the distance between us.

Watching out across the sea, I am eternally hopeful that I will see his ship sail over the horizon. I wish this with all my heart and being, but sadly, I know in my mind that this will never happen. Nonetheless, I made a promise and commitment to myself, night after night, to sit and wait – watching for his return.

My soul longs to have him here with me, or to be there with him. I can understand why it is impossible for him to be here with me, but I cannot understand why it is impossible for me to be there with him. I cannot understand, just because I was born a female, why I can not be a sailor and travel with him across the sea. For it does not matter to me where we are, as long as we are together.

The longing, the watching, the waiting, is so unbearable and so unnecessary. And, it makes me so sad to think about how much more unbearable it must be for my dear James. I, at least, am surrounded by my familiar homeland and I have the comfort of my family. James, on the other hand, is so isolated from everything and everyone he loves.

The light of the full moon is now dancing o'er the rippling dark sea. The white crests of the aggressive waves are now thunderously crashing into the rocks upon which I sit. The air is growing much colder now, so I tightly drape my shawl over the top of my head and down around my shoulders. How I wish it were the arms of my James I feel totally encasing me – instead of my old weathered shawl.

I should be heading back to my cottage now. I am sure mother and father are beginning to get anxious as to my safety. Although they worry about my everyday evening pilgrimage, they allow me the freedom to do what is beckoning my spirit to do so. Maybe my parents understand because if they were in my stead, they would be doing exactly as I am. Douglas and Vanora Mackenzie possess souls that are welded together as one – the same as James and me.

How lucky I have been in this life to have chosen parents that have not only taught me the meaning of true love, but have lived their lives as an example of the epitome of soulful love.

I hypnotically soak in the moon one last time this evening. I tightly shut my eyes and pray a patron saint's blessing on James. I pray that he will remain safe and warm, that his journey will soon be over, and that he will speedily return to me. But most of all, I pray that as he looks out over the depths of the ocean that he can taste the depths of my love, as I can taste and savor his love for me. I then open my eyes and send my prayer straight forward towards the moon – the same moon that James is beholding this exact moment. With the moon and stars as my lantern, I rise up and walk back toward my home. I smile a peaceful smile, truly contented, for I know in my heart that I have communed with James – yet another evening.

This morning the rays of the brilliant sun stream through the small window in my tiny room that I sleep in, streaming across my cot and awaken me from my deep sleep. I groggily lift my head to watch the smoky rays prancing across my wool patch quilt, as I think to myself, "This is going to be an exceptional day."

I love the early morning of a brand new day. It causes me to be reflective of the things I am grateful for, and it saturates me with a sense of peace. I cherish my tiny room, my patch quilt, my old wood floors, my porcelain basin and pitcher. I treasure the security and serenity my small room presents to me.

I really desire to lie here on my cozy cot for a few hours, but I know I must arise and begin my day of routine chores. I fold back my quilt, swing my feet out onto the cold wooden floor and walk over to my window. My dear friend is beating on my pane, anxiously waiting to bid me a good morning. I open the latch and push back my window, allowing his rays to reach in to greet me.

My first thoughts this incredible morning, as they are every morning, are of my dear James. Where is he? Is he safe? Did he have a peaceful nights sleep?

When will he return to me?

I quickly get dressed and slip outside to begin my daily chores. I am determined not to be late for my evening communion with James. The sun is ever so bright today that I scarcely notice the crisp chill in the air. My preoccupation of James causes me to focus even more diligently on my work. Every moment I accumulate, I want it to be spent with James.

Later in the afternoon, as I sit down to dinner with mother and father, I can't help but study their interactions with each other. I almost feel a tinge of guilt for intruding on their acts of intimacies. The look of intense longing and adoration in my father's eyes as he stares at my mother serving up our dinner – well – it almost makes me blush. My mother, acknowledging his look out of the corner of her eye, gives him a hasty wink in return – causing me all the more to speedily finish my dinner and run out of our home to my place at the bay.

The evening is still fresh as I seat myself upon my familiar rock. The sunset this evening is indescribable – a portrait gift from heaven. I treasure every moment of it, feeling my spirit quietly connecting with James's spirit. I can sense his presence so vividly, as if he is actually physically here with me – the smell of his skin, the warmth of his breath, the passion and love in his eyes. I want to stay here forever.

Upon arising this new morning, I get dressed preparing as usual to begin my usual chores. Father stops me as I head out the door of our cottage. "Daughter," he says, "I need you to ride to the village with your mother and me this morning."

It is a long journey into the village, and therefore, I earnestly do not want to go. I know the trip will set me back on my chores. Nevertheless, I would not question, nor, disrespect my father's wishes.

Discerning the look of displeasure in my face, father adds, "I will make sure your chores are taken care of upon our return." Hearing this, I immediately look forward to our trip. My father rarely takes a trip into the village, and even less frequently, do mother and I have the opportunity to go to the village. The change of routine is a pleasant welcome.

About two hours later our wagon rolls into town. We ride on through the village, stopping at the seaport on the opposite edge of town. Father hops out of the wagon and ties down the horses.

It just occurs to me that I am unaware of the reason we journeyed into town. Probably to pick up some farming or fishing supplies, no doubt. Father walks around to the side of the wagon and assists mother in getting down off the wagon. He then holds his hand up to assist me in getting down off the wagon. Looking down at his face I am puzzled by his silly, boyish broad smile. Glancing up ahead over his shoulder and down towards the old wooden pier – there he stands.

I freeze.

Am I dreaming? This must be a dream!

The sound of father belting out a gut-filled laugh startles me back to reality. This isn't a dream!

My James is home.

I vault off the wagon and run madly towards the pier – James already running vigorously towards me. I leap into his waiting, outstretched arms. Our bodies mesh together as he spins me around. Heart pressed against heart, I feel our spirits reconnecting. Once again we are united body, soul and spirit.

James slowly rests me down on the pier, our arms still tightly wrapped around each other. For what seems like an eternity, we silently stare deep down into one another's eyes – one another's soul. The silence is deafening. There is no one – no sound – around us. We are the only two souls in the universe. He lowers his face towards my face and tenderly places his lips on my lips. We kiss deeply, enduringly, passionately.

That evening as we sit huddled together on our rock; James snuggly binds us in our blanket, in order to combat the inescapable cold night air. Laying my head gently on his shoulder, we gaze out at the moon – our moon – watching it glimmer o'er the rippling dark sea. James delicately places my cheek in the palm of his hand and raises my face towards his.

To smell his skin, to feel the warmth of his breath, to see the passion and love in his eyes, to me – this is my heaven.

I want to stay here forever.

⌘ ⌘ ⌘ ⌘

I am an old woman now. My dear parents have been gone for many years. I buried my beloved James last Wednesday, up on the hill behind our cottage – among the wild flowers and the yellow St. John's Wort. He is gone from this world, but not from my spirit. I can still feel him here – deep down in my soul. It is as if he has never left me.

Even though James and I are always together, whether in the physical or not, I find I must be with him in the physical. I am too old and too tired to wait once again for our physical reunion. I don't have the energy and patience of the young lassie sitting by the dark bay in the moonlight.

I lie down on my bed, close my eyes and call out to James in my mind.

"James, my love. I need to be with you. Not just in spirit and soul, but also in body. Please, James, come and take me with you."

My soul rises above me, hovering near the roof of our cottage. I look back down at the discarded encasement lying on the bed.

Am I dreaming? This must be a dream!

Looking up – there is James. He lightly, but

firmly, tugs on my arm.

"No, my love. You are not dreaming."

"Let us go home – together."

~ ~ ~ ~ ~

To all you poor lassies,
From long ago shores
To mere tides of asteroids,
To fear the young lords
To spread across vessels,
To cross the large seas
May you rest among islands,
And fear no more lore

~ ~ ~ ~ ~

Chapter 11

Spiritual Fulfillment

Time constraints were created by man. The weight of life bore with it a heaviness of disarray. A longing for freedom kept man from progressing, monopolizing their existence and possessing their souls.

Chains of dissolution followed the way.

The Journey...

Breathe, just breathe, is all I remember upon entering this life.

High in the air is my home. For miles and miles all you can see is green. Jotting up to the skyline is tremendous mountains of rocks that surround us like a protective barrier. I knew immediately that I was special. I have memories of another time and place filtering through me. I am aware that it is another time and place, but yet, it seems immensely similar – almost identical. The faces are slightly blurred, but very recognizable.

I know I have a short time to enjoy this beautiful land that is so inspired by my own land, from whence I came. My family members are farmers. All the people in this region work very hard and long days. They love this land as they love their people.

It is their land. They were born here and they will be buried here for centuries to come.

The country can be the coldest of cruelest terrain, but when the beauty opens up – it swallows you whole and envelops your very senses.

I watch the mammoth clouds drift by, as I lay

on this ground starring into the blueness of the sky, and I view glimpses of who I am and who I was before I entered this plane. I think, knowingly, one day I will leave this region for a higher plane. I have so many answers, and just as many questions. Nonetheless, I know at my young age these questions and answers will be given the timely experience they need – and so will I.

But until then, I will enjoy this journey I am on.

I love my mother and my family here. Our life is a life of simplistic beauty. Our village is small, and everyone is familiar with everyone. We help each other make the day grow and end together. I love this life I am leading; however, I know there is more to come – much more.

One of my brothers is being sent away to learn a higher meaning to life. He is to learn of various cultures and the way of spirituality. The students will study the stars and the heavens, as well as their movements. They will learn about art and medicines that come from our earth. Many talents are being taught to them – talents unlimited.

The people of this region are courageous. Perhaps it comes from their deep held beliefs.

We live in peace and harmony. Nonviolence is our nature. We hold a reverence for all living things. All things, great or small, share no diversity.

We are all one and we are one with the universe. We are one with all beings – accepting everyone for his or her differences. We revere them for where they are on their journey in this life, and for where their journey is taking them.

I close my eyes as I lay here in a state of tranquility. I see another time and place. I see buildings. I see structures of enormous strength. I see a bird, a mother bird. I watch this mother bird that has an ideal nesting spot. It is a hole in the building where about four of the stones are missing. It is about thirty feet off the ground, and a good distance from the top of the structure.

Nothing can touch her.

Every time she takes a worm inside, she is completely out of sight. All you can hear is a distant chatter of happy baby birds, whenever she brings them a morsel of food. Six or seven times, I watch her come in and out of her perfect home. I am amazed to notice that every time she enters her high spot; she stops at the entrance and checks in all directions –

making sure it is safe to enter. She does not realize that she is living in one of the safest places in the world.

I think that is how *we* live. We are safe from the rest of the world. No harm can befall us.

I feel that safeness.

As I awake from this dream state, I look around and accept my surroundings with open arms. I long for my mother's breasts and feel a need to return home. Racing home, I pretend I am that bird, gently lifting from the ground and heavily returning with both feet. I am between the ages of three and four in these years. There is much thought looming through my mind.

As I reach my diminutive home, I can smell a delightful aroma exiting from the cooking quarters. My essence is illuminated. Hunger begins to amplify inside of me. I sit and wait impatiently for the taste of a meal.

While my mother serves me a morsel of fare, we look out towards the front of our home. Off in the distance we see three men approaching in the direction of our abode. This happens quite frequently. My mother often feeds travelers on their quest to the main city. She stands and begins to make tea for the new arrivals.

Mother graciously invites the men into our home for tea and a bite of food. I study the men curiously. Somehow – I know these men, but I can't identify why or how I know them.

Instinctively, I climb into the lap of the tallest man. He is wearing a hand carved medallion. I study the medallion inquisitively. He begins to ask me questions concerning the pendant.

"Do you know to whom the pendant belongs to?" he asks.

"Yes, I do," I respond.

I then tell them the name of the person to whom it had belonged. Everyone in the room is astonished. "Unbelievable!" they exclaim. Yet, all the while, it seems as though the men knew I had this knowledge. They tell my mother they had sought me out for this very reason.

Their journey had led them to me – to this time and place. They say I share a life with someone that had been here before, and I was born to help rule my people. They continue to say that I was here before and that I have returned to take my place at the head of the temple.

Sadly, I must leave my mother behind and go with them. Gratefully, my brother will be able to join me and keep me company.

I know I must go. This is my rightful destiny,

although, I will miss my mother immensely. No truer love can ever be found. My mother will have to release me from her side. She may come to visit me, but her visions of my future are forever changed – even simple visions. To give her child up to a higher purpose is a gift, though it may seem unbefitting at the time.

The New Journey...

As I open myself up to my true destiny, I encompass occasional setbacks of loneliness and misunderstanding.

My teachers at this new retreat are kind and compassionate. Nonetheless, to a small boy it is difficult to comprehend the emptiness I feel at times. This life has journeyed a long way. The mysteries are unveiling daily, as a song that is whispered by the lone bird. My vision of this place is to bring peace and unity to my people – and love thereafter.

In this tiny village where we live, it is becoming increasingly laborious to carry out this vision. Our neighbors to the east are finding it in their power to control and conquer our small country. I do not understand the hatred that stems from such actions. I am advised that I must leave this place that is inherent in me to identify as home.

Will justice serve us? We cry out for help, but alas, no one is answering.

We cannot fight these ministers of war. We are not combatant. It goes against everything we hold to be true. All we can do is hope for freedom. If freedom does not come within this lifetime, maybe it will come in the next. Perhaps this place we call home will flower and change – change into the dwelling we foresee in our minds.

⌘ ⌘ ⌘ ⌘

I will contest this altercation and containment with my last fading breath. I must free my people.

Yes, this is what I must do – only this.

Chapter 12

Circle Complete

As I stroll through my homeland with my dear friend, Leopold, at my side, the brilliance of his existence consumes my being. The tans and grays that spot his fur, cover him in a dazzling array of color that is delicately laced with bursts of white – which makes every movement he makes a picture in itself. His lush green eyes can be seen for miles, his massive head resting just below my shoulder. With each step he takes, the grass beneath his powerful paws stands upright in unison.

Leopold and I were always in sync. We are a part of each other. I could feel his presence on my journey to the plane – not always knowing who he was – but just knowing he was there.

He is my dear friend.

Others call him by a different name. To me he is Leopold.

Our adventure this day will take a turn. We will head back to the plane in our spirit form to help guide a connection we made on one of our visits. Side by side – stride for stride – Leopold and I come closer to the waters of the wall that separates our world from our sisterland. We build our spirits strong and full of god-force, taking with us as much as we can carry. We approach the ice-like wall in front of us, slowing seeing the waters' moving colors – unbeknown to the next world.

With my arm engaged around my friend's neck, we step through the water of colors. We feel a slight suction, in reference of a woman giving birth in this new land, heeding our calling and feeling our connections tighten as we head to our appointed destination.

As we ride on, we feel the tug of lost souls gripping at our spirits – souls who have yet to find their way home – souls who have forgotten their purpose and their direction home. Maybe we can gather some of them on our way home, after our mission is complete. It is difficult for these souls to identify with who we are. They are not open to acceptance, for they believe they are still alive and living on this plane. Their journeys will inevitably be fulfilled in time. The sorrow I am feeling is for these souls that cannot break loose – but I know they will in time.

The Journey...

As we enter into the home of our sibling, we feel vibrations long remembered. She was my daughter on this plane. And to her (Amanda), Leopold is her guide – her spirit guide. I only hope and pray that on this day, we will be able to help her pass in ease. You see, Amanda is seventy-seven years old, today. She has lived a full life. She was the first woman to be elected president in her native land. She always spoke the truth, relying on her own convictions. She never was a puppet. She was always genuine – quite unlike many of her predecessors.

Amanda did not always have it so easy. In her younger years, she tried very hard to be overly independent. She was often running into walls with a hard head. She worked diligently and faithful. Amanda is leaving behind a wonderful family, which may make her passing a laborious experience.

We begin walking through the familiar rooms that are reminiscent of times we shared here. This was my home on this plane. I passed it down to my beloved daughter. It is a good-sized home – not too large – but large enough.

It is an A-frame structure with two bedrooms, constructed mostly of glass. The loft overlooking the downstairs has a sitting room separating the bedrooms. The home is very open – including the downstairs – which has no walls separating the large kitchen from the even larger living room.

Aside from the house, there is the magnificent view of the mountains. It is the view of these majestic mountains that inspires the energy of the house to blossom. You can see the peaks in every turn of every room. I can feel the home welcoming me back for this short visit.

Somewhere close by, I can feel Amanda. My soul leaps in anticipation. We are connecting.

Leopold and I walk up the circle of stairs in unison. The spirit of the home shows us the way. As we ascend into the master bedroom, there sits Amanda in a chair next to the window. She is steep in meditation as she gazes at the countryside.

We enter her space. I sit next to her on the left and Leopold encircles on the right, then he lays his massive head in her lap.

An unseen protection.

Her spirit and mine are one again. It is

comforting for her vessel. Although her vessel is unsure where the comfort is coming from, she knows everything is going to be right this day.

The life she shared on this plane now encircles her being. Mostly the happiest times surface, but included are some sadder memories – which don't seem so sad now.

Our eyes connect as I feel her spirit penetrate the skin and stand on its own, again. Once more I see the dance of the little girl. The laughter of the holiday mornings; the rides we shared; the ups and downs of life's offerings; the great epoch of existence, which no being can take from us!

Alas, we embrace – with Leopold's smile and great powerful paws wrapped around us both!

We feel someone ascend upon the home. I look in her eyes and sense she wants to stay. A short knock on the door and, immediately, the door opens. We hear a voice call for grandmother. Slowly climbing the stairs is a young girl – probably eighteen or nineteen in years.

As she comes closer, I can see how extraordinary this moment is.

She is me! She is an exact copy of what I

was on this plane. I can feel a piece of my light living inside this young girl.

A complete circle!

What a remarkable honor to see with these eyes a cycle completed!

The young girl runs to the vestige that remains slumped over in the chair by the window. She lays her long brown hair on her lap. Amanda reaches out to her, but quickly pulls her hand back – knowing she cannot help her with her grief this day.

I stroke her hair hoping to break through the despair. She is very close to Amanda – closer than most. Maybe it is the resemblance, or, maybe it is her spirit. Farther down the road we will be here to give this girl a ride home.

The young girl stands up and looks around the room. She can feel our presence. It will be difficult for her not to feel the fellowship of this circle. All the lifetimes of the angels are rolled into one. Three spirits of the same vessel are experiencing a voyage unknown to many.

The girl spoke, "I love you, Granny – I will miss you." As she grabs a picture off the table beside the bed, I can see it is one of her and her grandmother, Amanda. We will stay as long as it takes for Amanda to discern she can leave.

The time has come. She gives one last kiss to her granddaughter. We then begin our journey home. Arising, I ask Amanda what name was given to her granddaughter.

"Karen," she answers. "The same as yours."

We hold tight and consume the scenery at hand. Mountain peaks splatter the snow. Evergreens overflow. Small lakes add breathtakingly dramatic views. At this level it is hard to tell where our homeland begins and this one ends.

Yet, we all know we are going home. Home again – to our beginnings of this journey.

Never before have we felt so prominent the tug of our heartstrings and the chains that tie us together, forever. We now realize we are forever connected – then, now and tomorrow. We're thankful for this joyful return home, and for many more to come.

It is good to be home.

⌘   ⌘   ⌘   ⌘

Arriving at home I sit with Leopold and Amanda. I discuss with her her journey and what holds the secrets of the plane. We discuss how beings have lost their way. We discuss the endless cycle of abuse (both physically and mentally), from generation to generation. We discuss how the abuse has taken its toll on the beings. They torture their children with ridicule and mistreatment. Don't they realize that children are the stepping stones of their society? They have so saturated them with negativity that it will be difficult for them to endure, and difficult for them to find a means of change.

Amanda is telling us of her granddaughter, Karen. She was brought up under strict command and with very little love. She had to take on the ideologies of her parents from a very early age. Karen had such a free spirit as a child, but after so many spankings and having her brain stuffed with religious ideologies that made no sense to her, she was burned out in her teenage years. She was on the verge of suicide.

Amanda said she took Karen in and comforted her. She allowed her to think freely and allowed her to find her spirit. Amanda taught her prayer and meditation. She taught her how to open herself up to the universe – allowing the force inside her to swallow all negativity.

Karen found her place on this plane, a place where she could be free and fulfilled. Steadfast – just as her force of god remains.

Someday these beings will understand that all religions were created on that plane, not created in our true homeland. For if there was a religion here in our homeland – what would it be? If you find yourself waking up on that plane in a country that has an uncontestable religion – is it the fault of you that you were born in that part of the plane? Or, is it your obligation to fulfill your parent's ancestry, not knowing the difference? If children are to be taught religion, they need to be taught of all religion. We all agreed, still contemplating all that was learned this day.

The mysteries of the plane can simply be concluded with love, unconditional love. A love for your sons, daughters, mothers, fathers and neighbors alike. The mystery stays the same. Why aren't they using the tool that can cure anything – including their own souls?

Maybe in time they can turn around their

universe and put it back into balance.
Free will – what will we do with it?

Chapter 13

Conclusion

At the end of the last century we began rebirthing our nature children into this plane, in favor of taking over the responsibility of renewing this world. With their knowledge and background in tact, we positioned these sprites into a moral environment. They were to grow and become compassionate caretakers of this home away from home. Whereas, creating a new beginning, nursing back to health a celestial sphere.

Now the time has come to fulfill this voyage we have made. We have come full circle. The understandings we have discovered here have peaked, and we have become incorporated into our systems. We've taken this journey as far as we can go. The connection has been made and completed on this plane that we now speak of as Earth.

Love has overcome the negative forces here. The time has been well spent. The voyage has been a long and trying one, but now – today – we have another place we can call home.

The changes on this Earth are forthwith happening. The gases in the air are swirling while dissolving retired particles into new ones. I can feel our souls being pulled from these tired vessels, being set free as they were intended to be. The seas and waterways are spinning and recycling all that is empty. The archaic remains we used to house our souls are drying up and replenishing the ground. A great cold fire is sweeping the land, dissolving wire, concrete and empty buildings. Boundaries that were set by humans are moving and rejoining their lands.

The air is becoming purified. With the hemisphere margins disappearing – you can see our first homeland. It is majestically vibrant and it is illuminating directly above us, where it always was – just a touch away.

The pride, the prejudices – all gone. Love has replaced hatred. Or, was it ever really hate? Could it just have been misconstrued awareness?

The religious and excluding organizations that tore people apart and separated their hearts – all gone.

The freedom of our love and longstanding relationships remain, as it always has – right within our grasp.

Chapter 14

Home

As this day enters into the next, I find myself filtered into the new homeland. I have been here before in this form that I need to take on, but alas, I will make my vision known.

The way of this world seems to be discontent. If I show the force of all of our oneness with the power to project to our beings – surpassing the stillness that lies inside – imagine the rejection of comforted blindness. Imagine instilling the power of belief through eyes unknown, reflecting an awareness of peace and stability.

What a blanket of prosperity! This rich mount of visionary dreams has the possibility of enabling the response of hypersensitivity and enhancing the viability of existing dreams of persuasion. Once delivered; once enabled; once perceived; the wholeness on this plane, which is an envisioned dream-state, will last beyond time and beyond sanction.

We are all instilled with a true self. It is a force that goes beyond creed and justification. It is timeless – industrious and envisioned – whether it be life, happiness or thoughtfulness. We have but a dream – an inkling of what we are to be, or become. A happiness of a vision so obscure – so far from reach – can be a blessing of sorts.

Believe in a realm of undisputed truth. Disguise it as a substance. Hide it as a barrier. Launch an inverse system of beliefs not known by any man. Feel complacent energies resting at the feet of disturbance, hollowed out by ignorance and a consensus of truth. Systematically encourage a regiment of prosperity into thoughts unknown.

By the sake of man, no one person has perceived the ignorance of humankind. Touch the mountain of the sanctuary. Clasp the systems of lesser men. Transform the vengeance of evil minds. Scatter a victor among you.

I bring this pod to you – only you. Voice my stay. Hang to the contrast of difference.

Believe in you; believe in me. Here you will find a uniqueness of substantial existence. Upon this I will stand. Upon you, I will watch and commend the being of which you are – of which you are to be on this land of prosperity. The mystery of the ages will be passed down this day. What enables the minds of days to come will be what conspires from this day forward – completion elevated above all.

Conspired ignorance, which entangles the thoughts of unprecedented events, lay at the feet of unsuspecting beings. Mold and adhere to the unequivocal truths, truths not to be unscathed, but to be used as a tool – a selfless tool. Lend a hand to the variables of life and freedom, unobstructed by the beginning of self and self-absorption. Wean the small and small-minded from a lifetime of affliction. Find a way out of hibernation, into the will of the free. Liberate the mind and the heart. By now, no man is inspired to be free – lest bring a savior to transcend all manner of thought to save you up to the purpose of your being, to bring your dreams into stability, to enlighten and advise, to spark the day of inheritance resting with you. Keep all manner of substance in balance. Seek exposure of quality masses, being not what might have happened, but insisting what could have happened.

Be alive – unbound by perpetual happiness in all things – unspotted and untapped.

Live fulfilled. Yesterday. Today. Tomorrow. Forever. Live not through me, but through you and the coming of light, as you leave the hollowness of home and the stillness of existence by way of dreams. Heed an epiphany of waves of tides to the unknown territories of the mind.

I stand here, not to block your way, but to share your way – to guide and to protect in uncertain waters. Would you not do the same for me? Were you not always there with me? Will we not always be as one, not in pieces – but whole? We are a system of love and reprise – forgotten long ago – but not gone.

The life led on this plane and the events inherited, could they have been different? Should they have been different? If the story was always the same and the tide washed the same way, would we – could we – have lived differently?

It was the dream of being alive!

We are embodied by the same inherent belief, which is, to love effectively enough in order to enrich another soul. How seemingly effortless and pure! Inside of me rests you; and inside of you rests me. It is a very simple concept – no more and no less. This life I led seemed at times to be harrowing, virtuous, incomplete, partly noble, and maybe, substantiated. Yet, the reality of life is hidden. It is obscured in the moment of understanding, the understanding of truth and knowledge. It is obscured not from the outside world, but from the inside world – the unknown.

What can be held in this hand when our time here is finished? It is what we hold in our heart. To win with never losing brings what gain? To fast with never having eaten, would not serve any purpose. To love with never having been loved, would seem extraneous.

I listen. The sounds from the hidden voice, here, are put to rest. From here, I go to where I came. I go to rest in the arms of my home. Never leaving – never staying.

Just to have been.

Epilogue

The beast that lies inside me is resurfacing again. Had it been that I thought it disappeared? Or, had I buried it deep enough to elude confrontation?

The possibilities are intimidating. I may never know the secrets within myself, the hidden dragons, and the force that pulls me to the left or to the right.

This day has started out as any other day. Small messages are signaling my brain to awaken, to get out of bed, to walk down the hallway into the bathroom and ultimately into the kitchen where my hands diligently make the morning coffee – all in a robotic state, as I do every morning.

Settling in, I worship this time of the day, before unrest signals my stillness to depart from me – the time when the monster within me allows me to know he is advancing out of hiding and all systems are go! This is the same monster that takes his sharp dagger and holds it to my back in order to get me through, yet, another day of mundane duties.

Can it be we all have our own beast within that coerces us through all sorts of fruitless activities, impelling us to go through the motions of endless rituals? But alas, finds us halfway through this life unaccomplished of anything that is substantial, causing us to feel empty and powerless to change our somewhat comfortable existence. All alone, except for the disquiet alarm imbedded within our intellect.

Who or what is it that lives within our hearts and minds? Is it a part of oneself and not a part at all? Perhaps it is only a created version of our ego, placed there by ourselves, in order to keep us from going astray – a self-contained entity that is fully automatic and self-propelled.

Do you think a god or force would send us here with absolutely nothing with which to guide us, or, send us here with a body that isn't able to heal itself? If our mission here is of a spiritual content, wouldn't obstacles such as, taking care of these vessels, only hinder and slow down our mission (not to say we don't need to slow down from time to time)? We can only believe that our god or god-force is of the highest technology.

We feel our travels here are very personal. It

is a voyage between you and your god-force, only.

Remember that we are sent here with everything that we need contained inside of us. Listening to that small still voice will take you everywhere you need to be. You can find inspiration in the smallest of places.

If you always only look on the outside of a person you will never see the inner true self of that being. Everyone possesses an exterior facade that is erected from a menagerie of experiences created over a lifetime – good and bad experiences alike. We all have them. They are experiences created in this world – not of the previous world. Experiences are what we wear – what we bear. We have to look past all the layers and layers of paper mache. Look deep down into the heart where the true life-force dwells, pumping the blood to the being.

It is difficult. It is like pulling off the paper mache after it has become dry. But, we have to do it - just as our god-force looks at us, deep down into our soul to what we were before this adventure began – not to discard our blanket of this life but to use it. Sometimes it is difficult and toilsome to see under all that paper and glue.

I cannot stress the fact that maybe, just maybe, we planned all of this. Maybe, just maybe, we planned all these lives and experiences we are to live.

With our memory banks erased, could we have left home to arrive on this Earth with just our souls connected to home? Maybe we were to experience this human existence with no recollection of our past to overcome and incorporate our findings of this venture – a venture we will share with everyone when we return. Could we have done this before? Could we have orchestrated similar experiments in different parts of the universe?

Scientific fact has proven the dinosaurs roamed this planet with early man. Maybe, just maybe, they were created here, without a spirit, as a pre-test. Perhaps that experiment failed, and so, we opened the earth and allowed that existence to be swallowed up. Maybe, in order for us to expand our learning capabilities, we traveled here ourselves.

You have to believe there is more going on around us that we cannot explain. Needless to say, it still exists. Maybe, just maybe, there are thousands of experiments going on everywhere – even in other universes.

Dare to open your minds and hearts.

Question and explore your inner self and leave behind some of your beliefs and trained thinking.

We question our beliefs and what we hold to be true on a daily basis. Where did this information come from? Did we learn this? From whom did we learn it? Does it hold water? Are we conditioned – especially in our religious beliefs – an area of our lives that is suppose to be the most open and free? What have we done here? What have we accomplished?

We seem to be so barbaric. Look around you, what do you see? Electrical lines, telephone poles, large buildings, massive weapons – it's almost comical. This is what we have accomplished over thousands of years?

Question yourselves. Question your motives. Question your belief system. Question your life force inside of you.

Do it daily.

If you must, throw away everything you were brought up to know and believe. Afterwards, choose a new path between you and your god-force, and you will find your way on the path you were born to take.

It is time to take charge of our world.

It just seems so lunatic for humans to be

sending spaceships loaded with plutonium on a seven year journey, or for park officials to be dumping poison in a bay in California in order to kill a certain species of fish – along with everything else in the bay.

I can't believe we are still in this frame of mind. Moreover, it is all done in the name of technology. Ha!

We have become a world of robots. We go through life doing and saying whatever we are told to do or say. We have spent a huge percent of our time using brut force in criminal activity, wars, disciplining our children, etc., which brings us to the human side – violence breeds violence – that simple. Maybe we haven't ventured as far from the spiritless Neanderthal creatures as we think.

What would make an eleven-year-old and thirteen-year-old boy shoot down their classmates and teacher? So unthinkable. Were they ignored by the people around them? Were they thrown into a melting pot of personalities and opinions? Were they ridiculed and discarded because they didn't fit "the mold"?

It is so sad that the souls that were entrusted to us are now gone, sent back early, or are rotting in prisons.

What are we teaching our children? If they learn by example, are we teaching them to become zombies? We rise every morning to go to work or school. We return in the evening to sit in front of a television or computer. We fret over money matters, possessions and trivialities. What have we done with our knowledge – with our love?

We've stowed it away with our greed – not just greed of money and possessions – but greed of self-centeredness.

Do you think we came here to watch television? Do you think we came here to collect possessions and to build our fortunes?

We went full circle into the human side of this existence.

What happened?

When did this experiment on Earth go array?

Our lives are difficult because we choose to have difficult situations litter our existence. We choose to experience every characteristic of life –good and evil – but to only touch the very least inside of evil and to slowly walk away. We choose to find out the true meaning of love. We choose to love the thunder and rain, the flies, the hornets and the little snake at our feet. We choose to understand their worth, their purpose for our existence and our understanding.

Why are we here? Are we alien? Many people have claimed to be abducted by aliens. They insist they are taken and examined without pain. Maybe it is our ancestors returning to check up on these vessels.

Who knows?

Have we another life or lives that we have no recollection of? Are we actually here physically on this planet Earth? Or, are we playing out parts of dreams that seem real enough, mere molecules floating in a dream sequence and staying only for short periods of time – unlocking small doors and picking up tiny parts of relevant information – then going on to our next dream?

If everyone could become in tune with these aspects of this life, we could maybe step up to a higher consciousness – be it ever so slight. We might not even notice at first, but it would be there…quietly there.

When will this dream end? When will we wake up?

Today? Hopefully – today.

⌘ ⌘ ⌘ ⌘

We imagine ourselves being older – maybe in our eighties – rocking in rocking chairs on my redwood deck, on the back of my old white farmhouse. No more desperation, no more frantic efforts to make something happen. Being relaxed with who we are and what we are to become. Being comfortable with the unknown. Playing out our lives in ease.

Having a good dream.

Recommended Reading

8 Weeks To Optimum Health...*by Andrew Weil, M.D.*

Anatomy Of The Spirit...*by Caroline Myss*

Change Your Thoughts –...*by Dr. Wayne Dyer*
Change Your Life

Discovering Your Soul Mission...*by Linda Brady &*
Evan St. Lifer

Many Lives, Many Masters...*by Brian Weiss*

More Than Meets The Eye...*by Yvonne Perry*

Proud Spirit...*by Rosemary Altea*

Something More...*by Sarah Ban Breathnach*

The Findhorn Garden...*by The Findhorn Community*

The Jesus Mysteries...*by Timothy Freke & Peter Gandy*

The Seat Of The Soul...*by Gary Zukav*

The Temple Gate...*by Mark Antony Wray*

What If God Were The Sun?...*by John Edward*

References

Grolier Encyclopedia Of Knowledge
Grolier, Inc. 1993
Danbury, CT   Volume 6
Dan-Ele

The World Of Dalai Lama
Gill Farrer Halls 1998
copyright Quest Books

Printed in the United States
100841LV00001B/5/A

9 781432 716486